P
MW00472094

The Potter and the Clay

"It is with great joy that I give my highest recommendation for this impactful book, *The Potter and the Clay*. This riveting story of a tragic life, countered by the faithfulness and love of God, serves as a life preserver for many who are sinking in the murky waters of hopelessness. This is the sort of story I would gladly recommend as a source of encouragement for the prodigal and those waiting for them to return home. Ellis's story is raw, yet compelling; it reaches down to the gutter of human despair and rises to height of divine providence. In my opinion, the story of Ellis Lucas is a timely resource for healing and restoration for today's lost and broken generation."

Pastor Al Pittman
Calvary Worship Center
Colorado Springs, Colorado

"I am truly honored to be asked to give my recognition to this riveting book. What an amazing testimony giving what I like to call good old fashioned "shoe-leather" theology. It brings to life the truth of God's word in Isaiah's prophesy, "God will give them beauty for ashes, The oil of joy for mourning, The garment of praise for the spirit of heaviness; That they may be called trees of righteousness, The planting of the LORD, that He may be glorified" (NKJV Isa 61:3). Ellis' testimony not only describes beautifully God's amazing love, mercy and grace towards us, but His unfailing, sustaining power as He holds on to us, molds us and shapes our lives into the vessel He has created us to be. It is a must read for those who might feel as though they are damaged beyond repair. Jesus is not only in the business of salvation but also renovation. He is always there with open arms to receive us the way we are, but loves us too much to leave us that way. He is so worthy, not only of our praise, but of our surrender to His shaping."

Pastor Scott Gurwell
Calvary Chapel of Liberty
Liberty, Missouri

"Ellis' story is hugely impacting and will help those who are hurting from past and present abuse to understand that God loves them and is still at work in their lives to bring healing and hope."

Victor Marx
All Things Possible Ministries; The Victor Marx Story: When Impossible is the Only Way Out.

"The title of Ellis Lucas' book, *The Potter and The Clay*, I thought pretty much summed it up: "A story of a lump of mud, we call humanity, that is transformed into something beautiful and useful by a creative potter." However, after reading I found it to be much more than that! There is power in a personal life changing testimony. There is hope in knowing that we are not alone in the trials and challenges we may face. There is encouragement for those that feel hopeless and helpless. Ellis' story is one that will resonate with wayward prodigals and worrisome parents. I highly recommend spending time with this book and reflecting on your own relationship with the Potter."

David Lin
Lead Singer - 9TH Hour
Nehemiah Fest
Smithville, Missouri

"This book shows the love and grace of God in a person's life. After reading this book, I feel it can be a great help to many Christians and those struggling with becoming a Christian (accepting Christ as their Savior and Lord). This book describes how a loving God has taken time to make sure we know His love for us and how He puts people in our lives to help draw us to Him. It also shows how God uses difficult circumstances to demonstrate His magnificent work. Ellis's testimony shows how God can use anyone, no matter what they have done in their past, and glorify Himself. We may not have experienced what Ellis has, but because of his testimony, we too can look back and see how God's grace has been working in our lives. *"And we know that all things work together for good to them that love God, to them who are the called according to His purpose (Romans 8:28)."* I recommend this book for everyone, no matter what his or her spiritual walk is like. For those who may be in doubt about God's love for them and for the seekers: God is there and ready to bring you into His family."

Pastor Wayne Titus
Valley Community Church
Rapid City, South Dakota

"Knowing Ellis as a man sold out to right living, as one who spends his entire life to help others, that's one thing. Then to read his story—to glimpse backward into the broken mess of the first chapters of his life--that's another. He is an entirely different man now! The contrast is spectacular. The catalyst for this truly radical change is stunning. Whatever interrupted him is worthy of a look. If your life needs a touch on the reset button, here's a story for you. Believe me, Jesus works. I've seen evidence. His name is Ellis."

Lori Harris
Recording Artist
www.loriharris.com
singitloud, singitproud

"It is my great honor to recommend this book. Life many times takes us down a road to addiction, loneliness, emptiness, and sadness. It spirals out of control and then we find ourselves in a place of no return! But Ellis tells us in his book how he finds hope, peace, love and life. How his life now has purpose. It happened when he gave his life away and began to obey the one that could reshape him. Everyone should read this book and give one to someone who needs some hope in their life."

Rev. John Mohler
Chaplain Missouri Bikers for Christ
Sr. Pastor Mt. Pleasant Baptist Church
Norborne, Mo

*The Potter
and the Clay*

The Potter and the Clay

Hard-Pressed on Every Side, but Not Destroyed

Ellis Lucas

PEARL PRESS

ISBN-13: 978-0-9896792-3-7
LCCN: 2014902789

Cover Design by James Arneson
Typeset by Mary Kristin Ross

Printed in the United States of America

Dedication

I would like to dedicate this book to one of my very best friends apart from my wife Peggi, and my dear Lord and Savior Jesus Christ, my Dad, Delbert Dean Lucas, and, to my late mother, Mary Jeanette Lucas, who was to me a true and faithful witness unto God, a remarkable reflection and portrait of the love of Jesus Christ. And to the memories of three wonderful prayer intercessory ladies who have all recently went home to be with Jesus, where they have each received their eternal rewards for their faithful service unto God. Three magnificent ladies who prayed for me continually and loved me as one of their very own and whom much like my own mother; will live on forever in my heart: Maxie Irwin, Madeline Hatfield, and Phyllis Combs. And then finally, I would like to dedicate this book to my beautiful wife Peggi Sue, and, to Peggi's and my children: Mandy, John, Latisha, Alissa, and Michael.

Sincerely,

Ellis Lucas

Contents

Foreword

Oftentimes when asked to write a foreword for a book that involves a person's personal memoirs, you agree to do it with a certain foreboding, thinking it is simply going to be another boring repertoire of somebody's life, from birth to their present age, of events that are of interest to them and members of their family but of little or no interest to anyone else. However, nothing could be further from that notion than this book, *The Potter and the Clay*. I have known Ellis for about ten years, and he is a dear brother in Christ and a very dear friend. I was not fully cognizant of his life's testimony of coming to Christ and the walk he has had with the Lord since then for the past several years, but I can tell you without any equivocation that his memoir is one of the most powerful testimonies I have read in a very long time of God's supernatural, gracious, merciful, and powerful work in someone's life.

I was deeply moved by many of the stories he presented in his book, but the one that gripped me the most was the account of his friend Mark Webb coming to Christ, and all the things God taught Ellis through that experience. Indeed, those truths of not discounting anyone from coming to Christ are essentially important for all of us! In addition, the accounts of God's deliverance of him from going to prison, as well as from his $41,000 IRS debt, are incredibly important for all of us in realizing that God is our source, and as we surrender to Him, He *"is able to do exceeding abundantly beyond all that we ask or think, according to the power that works within us, to Him be the glory in the church and in Christ Jesus to all generations forever and ever. Amen (Ephesians 3:20–21)."* And finally, the honesty of Ellis in revealing his struggles that we all have as believers in Jesus Christ was wonderfully refreshing, as he showed God's great love and grace in all areas of his life, including his courtship and marriage to his beautiful wife, Peggi.

Therefore, with a deep sense of gratitude for even being asked to write this foreword, I enthusiastically recommend this book to all who want to see an example of the depth of God's transforming grace and mercy in a person's life, as well as to be greatly encouraged to know that our God is indeed *"the same yesterday and today, yes and forever (Hebrews 13:8),"* and as He did with Abraham, Moses, Peter, and Paul, so too He did with Ellis, and He will do the same for you if you let Him. And I especially want to encourage those of you who have never accepted Jesus Christ as your Lord and Savior to read this book and know that whatever your personal struggles, addictions, failures, and criminal acts may be, Jesus not only can, but greatly desires to, set you free and bring you into His abundant life, just as He did with Ellis and is continuing to do every day of Ellis's life, as he describes in his book.

And for any and all believers who are struggling with your walk with the Lord, who have experienced personal failures and great disappointments in your Christian life, please take comfort and counsel from the Holy Spirit as you read Ellis's book that as God has done for him, so too will He do for you: *"And we know that God causes all things to work together for good to those who love God, to those who are called according to His purpose. For whom He foreknew, He also predestined to become conformed to the image of His Son, that He might be the firstborn among many brethren; and whom He predestined, these He also called; and whom He called, these He also justified; and whom He justified, these He also glorified. What then shall we say to these things? If God is for us, who is against us? He who did not spare His own Son, but delivered Him up for us all, how will He not also with Him freely give us all things? Who will bring a charge against God's elect?*

"God is the one who justifies; who is the one who condemns? Christ Jesus is He who died, yes, rather who was raised, who is at the right hand of God, who also intercedes for us. Who shall separate us from the love of Christ? Shall tribulation, or distress, or persecution, or famine, or nakedness, or peril, or sword? Just as it is written, 'For Thy sake we are being put to death all day long; We were considered as sheep to be slaughtered.' But in all these things we overwhelmingly conquer through Him who loved us. For I am convinced that neither death, nor life, nor angels, nor principalities, nor things present, nor things to come, nor powers, nor height, nor depth, nor any other created thing, shall be able to separate us from the love of God, which is in Christ Jesus our Lord (Romans 8:28–39)."

God bless you as you read this book.

Justin T. Alfred Word in Life Ministries

Murrieta, CA

Acknowledgments

There are so many people I want to acknowledge for making this book so special to me and for their love and support throughout the different stages of my Christian life.

First of all, I want to acknowledge my Lord and Savior Jesus Christ and give thanks to Him for all the great things He has done in my life. For the price He so willingly paid with His own flesh and blood and the suffering He endured on the cross at Mount Calvary that paved the way for the miracle that set me free and the love that healed and restored my shattered life, thank you, Jesus! Also to Jesus for blessing my life with such an amazing and precious wife, Peggi Sue. *Proverbs 18:22 (NKJV): He who finds a wife finds a good thing, and obtains favor from the LORD.*

I want to say thank you to my wife, Peggi, for all the hard work she did with the editing of this book and for the research she did in finding long-lost records and documents that helped with the writing of this book. I also want to say thank you for your never-ending support in the ministry our God has called us to; I love you more than life itself!

I want to say thank you to my dear friend and brother in Christ, Justin Alfred, for being such a faithful and courageous friend throughout the different stages of my Christian life, always there to offer advice and counsel in love, enabling me to keep my eyes and heart fixed on Jesus Christ through the dark days and testings of my life, and for writing such an appropriate and timely foreword for this book. Peggi and I are so grateful to your entire family for all your love and support. We love you all very much!

I want to say thank you from the bottom of my heart to my pastor, Al Pittman, for writing such an amazing recommendation for this book and for extending such wonderful love, friendship, and support to both Peggi and me since our arrival to the Calvary Worship Center. We love you and Norma dearly.

Thank you to my great friend and fellow board member, Pastor Wayne Titus, and his precious wife, Sharron, for their love and support and for writing his recommendation for this book. May God continue to bless you both in furthering the gospel through the work being accomplished at the Valley Community

Church there in Rapid City, South Dakota; we love you both very much!

Thank you to my precious brother in Christ, Mark Webb, for lending his support to the writing of this book and for filling both Peggi's and my hearts with both love and affirmation. Peggi and I are forever grateful to you, and we're proud of the work God has done in shaping you into the man and servant of God you have become. Love you, buddy!

Finally, I want to acknowledge my precious friend and brother in Christ, Rick Simbro, and say thank you for being your brother's keeper! There are no words in the English vocabulary to adequately express my love and appreciation for the sacrifice you gave on my behalf.

Greater love has no one than this, than to lay down one's life for his friends (John 15:13 NKJV). Thank you, Rick, for everything. I love you more than you'll ever know!

and death, seasons of joy and pain, countless trials and difficult circumstances, including years of drug and alcohol abuse, depression, divorce, the loss of my three children, and then ultimately complete hopelessness. a life so completely destroyed I had come to believe there was absolutely no hope of ever changing and all I had to look forward to was whatever awaited me beyond the grave—most likely judgment. That was until March 6, 1997, while locked up in the Clay County Missouri Jail, at the end of life as I knew it, when Jesus Christ stretched out His mighty hand of grace and showed Himself along with an astonishing revelation that changed my life forever. God loved me and had an amazing plan for my life if I would open my heart and receive Him that day. It was a remarkable experience that I have documented in detail in the pages of this book as a testimony to the love, power, and grace of God Almighty, and over time I came to understand there is no human life beyond God's infinite desire and passion to love and to know, and no situation, pain, sin, or failure beyond His desire to forgive, heal, and restore.

After reading my story, I believe that many hurting souls will discover, as I have, the true meaning of "Clay in the Potter's hands," and how much the Master Craftsman cares for His creation! God knows, without my mother's love and sacrifice, I would have been gone for good, buried deep within the pit of hopelessness, damned to an eternal conscious existence, forever separated from Him and family. But Jehovah God, "The Master Potter and creator of all things," being rich in mercy, abounding in love, was determined to not let that happen, no matter how bad the vessel was broken or how filthy the jar had become. Amen! So before we begin this journey together, let me first offer up a short prayer for you, the readers, along with a very pertinent and appropriate passage from the Bible that I think explains it best according to what transpired in my life and is documented in the pages of this book. May God richly bless you all!

"Gracious heavenly Father, I come to you in the name of Jesus to petition Your throne of grace to use this testimony, the testimony that you gave me, to shine the light of your eternal hope and glory into the hearts, minds, and souls of whoever reads this book. Father, give strength to those having family troubles and power to the faint to keep trusting and believing Your Word as it pertains to their situations. Remind each one that there is Victory to overcome this current world as we are Your workmanship created in Christ Jesus for the magnificent purpose for which we were created (Ephesians 2:10)! Thank You for the lives this story will touch and I pray it all in Jesus' name. Amen!

"'Arise and go down to the potter's house, and there I will cause you to hear My words.' Then I went down to

the potter's house, and there he was, making something at the wheel. And the vessel that he made of clay was marred in the hand of the potter; so he made it again into another vessel, as it seemed good to the potter to make (Jeremiah 18:2–4 NKJV)."

1. Don't Let the Sun Set on Your Anger

I want to begin this journey with a brief look back into history at the book's original purpose, and how it all came to be, and say thank you to everyone for taking time to read my story. The book originally began as a letter to my son, written with my three biological children in mind, but along the way it became evident that God may have a far greater purpose in mind, as the original manuscript began to strike a nerve with many people, most being complete strangers. (I tell people today this really isn't my testimony; it belongs to Jesus Christ, the author and finisher of both my faith and my life (Hebrews 12:2).) He is the Potter and I am the clay, and He alone deserves the praise, glory, and honor for what He has been able to accomplish with my life!

It all started in the winter of 2011 after suffering a torn Achilles tendon and left gastronomies muscle while making a delivery at work in Colorado Springs. I was off work nearly three months rehabbing my injuries, and it was during that time that I began to think about my three children, two of whom I had not seen or heard from for nearly a quarter of a century, as they had all been adopted by their mother's third husband at a young age, leaving a painful scar burned deep into the tablet of my heart that never would heal. I truly believe God allowed the injury to accrue and may have even caused it for this reason. Earlier that year, in the spring of 2011, I received an unexpected call from my oldest daughter, who had been living in Southern California for the past several years, asking for help, explaining her situation, the situation of my two younger children and grandchildren. It wasn't good news, and it devastated my heart to learn. I had always prayed for my kids, though I hardly even knew them, but that particular call stirred my heart, changing everything, and from that moment on I began to cry out to Jesus like never before on their behalf, desperate to help in whatever way I could. I had had so many thoughts rushing through my mind since her call, coupled with all kinds of strange emotions, all the while at a complete loss for any sort of direction or answers as to what I should do. I was confused and scared, and a part of me just wanted to run and hide, not knowing what I could possibly do after all these years of being completely shut out of their lives.

However, it was during that time that the Lord began to take me back to the different spiritual markers in my own life, reminders of where I, too, had been held captive, to remind me of what it was in my life that shattered those gates of bronze and cut the bars of iron asunder. Psalm 107:16–20 describes the person I used to be before surrendering my life to Jesus Christ. I was a fool because of my transgression, a prisoner in chains and misery because of my rebellious ways. I was afflicted in every way and on every side because of my iniquity and, by all accounts, the least deserving of God's eternal love or salvation. However that didn't stop God from pursuing a meaningful and lasting love relationship with me, and in time, I could honestly say as King David did: *"It is good for me that I was afflicted, that I may learn Thy statutes (Psalm 119:71 NASB77)."*

The Bible says this: love bears all things, believes all things, hopes all things, and endures all things, and where these four characteristics exist, love never fails (1 Corinthians 13:7–8). Without a doubt, it was the unfathomable love of God, manifested and lived out in the lives of my mother and many others that ultimately laid claim to the victory that allowed me to overcome this evil world. And I truly believe that my story may help unlock the doors to my children's freedom as well.

So the purpose behind my writing this book is to record a story with evidence so compelling and powerful that, in the words of Josh McDowell, it absolutely demands a verdict as to the existence of an all-loving, all-powerful, all-knowing God and to the validity of His holy word. I truly believe God has purposed in His heart to share this story as a testimony to not only my biological children, but also to a lost and hurting world to provide answers, solutions, and direction to those who have ears to hear and hearts to believe, and this is the reason I felt so compelled to tell my story. *"And they overcame him by the blood of the Lamb and by the word of their testimony (Revelation 12:11a NKJV)."* I, like many others, had a great start in life, with all the potential to be anything I set my mind to be; that is, had I made better choices at critical times during my adolescent years and chose a different path through the stormy seasons of severe testings that came my way, and then sought experienced counsel from godly people who could have provided wise guidance through those painful seasons of my early years.

However, when I was a child, not nearly as much was known about childhood adolescence, and hardly anything was taught in the public schools about how it affects the social developmental behavior in a person's life. Today, after all the domestic violence and senseless killings in our public schools and other places, much more time has been rendered to the study of childhood adolescence to see what, if any, connection there may be in all those senseless acts of violence. Most studies conclude that to better understand adolescents in society depends on multiple perspectives from such areas as psychology, biology, history, sociology, education, and anthropology. Within these perspectives, adolescence is viewed as a transitional period between childhood and adulthood, whose cultural purpose, according to these studies, is the preparation of children for adult roles. Studies also show that between the ages of ten and twenty-five years old, the brain undergoes multiple changes that have important implications for human behavior, which coincidentally just happens to be the window of time where my life began to implode and come unraveled. I do believe there is some truth to the conclusion of those various studies, but I take issue with one thing: that none of those studies made any mention of the Bible and what it has to say about the difficulties of childhood adolescence. And as I have discovered, without the Bible, there are no adequate answers or solutions to childhood struggles or the ongoing pressures of childhood adolescence. The only trustworthy answers are the ones recorded in the Holy Bible. *Train up a child in the way he should go, and when he is old he will not depart from it* (Proverbs 22:6).

I was nine years old when our family moved from the family farm at Lathrop, Missouri, where I was well adjusted and well on my way to becoming a normal and productive member of society, to the small town of Stanberry, Missouri. It was a definitive turning point in my life and the beginning of a twenty-four-year downward spiral that nearly cost me my life and my eternity in heaven before it was all said and done. Satan hates families, and especially children, and one of the most effective ways to destroy a family is to ruin a beautiful child created in the image and likeness of God. We live in dangerous times when demonic strongholds intensify with each new generation as we gravitate closer and closer toward the end of this particular age or dispensation in world history, and like the Bible predicted thousands of years ago, evil men and imposters continue to grow worse and worse, deceiving and being deceived (2 Timothy 3:13). I found myself swept away by a demonic deception so powerful I no longer recognized the person in the mirror by my mid-teens or, better yet, remembered the person I used to be as a child.

By that time I was so bitter and depressed that I lost all sense of direction and my heart was hard as stone. I began to resent my dad with a boiling passion and blamed him for everything that ever went wrong in my life, mostly because of the move and the negative effect it had on my young life. At age nine, the level of development in my mind suggested that if he really cared, he'd move us back to the farm and out of harm's way where we belonged, and to not do that would suggest he really didn't care at all. And the older I got, the worse things became. I hated my life. It felt like I was locked up in some mental prison, depressed out of my mind, with absolutely no end in sight or possible way of escape, at least that I could see at the time. To me, life was hopeless. I saw absolutely no hope or future for me at all, but I was terrified at the thought of dying. I knew if what my mom believed and taught was true, I would perish if I died in that condition. I was tormented by the thought of spending forever in hell, to which some of you might very well relate.

By my late twenties, I had almost gone completely mad, and then when I was about to turn thirty, things got worse. I found out my mother, whom I was very close to, had terminal cancer and had only six months to live. I went to pieces. I begged God to leave her and take my dad instead. I couldn't bear the thought of her dying and having Dad as my only parent. I was scared beyond words and felt completely alone, storm-tossed with no comfort at all. I knew this was more than I could handle and that my life would soon end, too, if I didn't get a handle on things soon.

▽ *Not the thing to pray!*

I felt completely unwanted and unloved by my dad. I thought he loved my three sisters but hated me.

I began to drink alcohol heavily, mostly beer, but after some time that wasn't enough to kill the pain, so I began drinking Jim Beam whiskey along with beer. It only got worse as I turned to cocaine and then meth, which soon left me incapacitated and unable to work. Within two years of trying to survive that kind of pain, my wife at the time moved to New Mexico to live with her mom. I never blamed her. I could no longer help myself, let alone take care of her, and none of it was her fault. She did the best she could for a lot longer than most people could, but she could no longer deal with my situation. I was bitter and so full of hatred and rage that she knew it was hopeless to stay any longer, and we both knew things would get worse before, or if, they were ever to get better.

The next three years were the worst. You've heard it said, "It's darkest just before the dawn." Well, I had no idea just how dark it was going to get before it got better. I moved from Springfield, Missouri, north to my dad's farm where he had an old, abandoned farmhouse that no one had lived in for quite some time. It was all run-down and raggedy, but I had nowhere else to go, so it would have to do. Dad had agreed to let me stay there temporarily until I could figure out what to do with my life. It was a nasty old house, and the only source of heat was an old wood-burning furnace in the basement. The basement wall on the north side had partially caved in, and it was just a matter of time before it fell in completely.

Then not long after I moved in, a cat showed up in the front yard that looked just like the cat my wife and I used to have. I hated it coming around, because it reminded me of her and everything I lost from all those years of rebellion and stupidity. I tried to run it off, but it just wouldn't go. I finally got so angry that I went to Dad's house one morning to get a gun and kill the cat, but that didn't work either. For some reason, I could not hit the cat. I would aim carefully but could not hit that cat no matter how hard I tried. This went on for days until one day, I snapped out of pure frustration, and rage began to take over.

At that point in my life, I had so much anger boiling inside me that I could have killed a person under the right circumstances, not on purpose, but through a blind rage. I was definitely out of control. I never was able to kill that cat, though. In fact, one night while in the basement of the old house, drinking a bottle of Jim Beam and poking around at the wood stove, a giant rat came out from behind the woodpile and sat down in the middle of the floor and stared at me. I freaked! I didn't know what to do except go get the gun and shoot it. The problem was it would never come out when I had the gun. I finally decided I had no other choice but to get the cat and put her in the basement in hopes that she might kill the rat. Well, believe it or not, I never saw the rat again, "thank God," and after that, the cat somehow became my best and only friend.

Not too long after that, my dad tried to help by buying me a very nice used car. He thought it might give me a boost in my confidence and maybe rescue me from the wicked depression that was crippling my life. However, it only made things worse. I went on a drinking and drugging binge, and within four hours of taking possession of that beautiful car, I hit an embankment head-on at seventy miles an hour, flipping it end over end through a corn field. After that I knew I couldn't win, and I began to lose all hope. I was taken to a nearby hospital by the county sheriff and treated for my wounds and then woke up alone two days later on the couch at that old house, badly bruised, with a sore back, and cut to pieces, but otherwise fine.

I was afraid, however, that I may have been charged with a DUI (Driving Under the Influence) and would lose my CDL (Commercial Driver's License) and never drive a truck again, which was the only way I knew to make money. However, and to my surprise, the police report said there were no drugs or alcohol involved. I thought, "No tickets. Are you kidding?" I was shocked; I knew I was wasted on a variety of different drugs and alcohol when I crashed, but what's really weird was the actual wreck. I remember hitting the bank and flying through the air and all the while knowing I was having a horrible wreck, but everything was happening in slow motion. It was a strange sensation that seemed to last a lifetime; however, I don't remember hitting the ground and landing on my top, or the two days that followed. What I do know is this: there was a definite reason why I wasn't killed that night and why I never got a DUI, as you will see later in the book.

However, things would get much worse before they got better. Two months later at that old house, some party friends came out to watch a football game. One of the guys went to the basement to check on the fire and filled the stove with the wrong kind of wood. I had a stack of hedge wood that burns extremely hot and is very dangerous if used the wrong way. I would use a few chunks on the bitter cold nights to mix with other wood to make a warmer fire. That would keep the house warm on those extremely cold nights. My friend filled the stove full with hedge. He didn't know any better; wood was wood to him. I heard it popping and cracking and knew something was wrong. I went to the basement and saw what he had done. I pulled the hedge out of the stove and replaced it with oak, and everything looked fine at the time, but it wasn't. At two a.m. the next morning, I was awakened by the same cat I tried to kill running up the back of the couch I was sleeping on, jumping down and sinking all four claws into my stomach. I was stoned out of my mind at the time, and when I did come to, there were flames all around me. The house was on fire and burned completely to the ground that night, almost taking my life with it. There was nothing left but a pile of ashes, charred wood, and one small room at the northeast end of the house that was spared. That was where I kept my family keepsakes my mother set aside for me before she died, which I still have today. I immediately knew why I couldn't kill the cat. God sent that cat and protected it for that very purpose, to keep me from perishing that night in a blazing inferno. I know now there was a deadly spiritual war being fought over my soul. Satan was determined to destroy me, but little did he know that what he meant for evil against me, God was using for my good.

Looking back now, I clearly understand I was simply being washed with the Launderer's soap and refined in the Refiner's fire (Malachi 3:2), and had it not been for the amazing grace of God and the sacrifice of Christ, I would not be here today to tell this story. It was the day after Thanksgiving that the house burned down, and it was an early winter in northwest

Missouri. There were six inches of snow on the ground, and I had nowhere to stay. At that point I was both homeless and helpless. I hear people say, "God helps those who help themselves," but I have no idea where they get that idea from, because it's nowhere to be found in scripture, and the truth is, as I have discovered, God helps those who cannot help themselves. He is the ultimate giver of grace, and I'm so grateful He is, because I had a long hard, uphill climb ahead.

At that point I really couldn't stay with Dad, and no other family wanted anything to do with me, so I decided it would be best to stay with a girlfriend until the spring. That, however, didn't work out so great either. I became extremely paranoid while staying at her house and nearly lost my mind completely. Her former husband had worked for my dad but was killed in a car wreck a year and a half earlier. Then she had a boyfriend living with her who was shot and killed in her front yard by an angry neighbor who was never convicted nor did he do any time for the murder of that young man. She and I would stay up daily doing drugs late into the night and hardly ever slept, and I was starting to have weird feelings that I, too, would die if I didn't get out of there soon.

I was beginning to show signs and have symptoms very similar to schizophrenia that were no doubt caused by or, at least in some way, directly related to

▽ the years of hard drug and alcohol abuse, and I could no longer discern what was real from what was not. I knew that life as I knew it was coming to an end and that time was running out on me; my body and mind could no longer endure the alcohol and chemical abuse and going days without sleep. I needed to get out of there, and I needed to get out fast. I was not ready to die, but the road I was on was the pathway to destruction, and deep down, I knew it. I was in desperate need of help if I was going to survive, and, in fact, Tammy, the girl I was staying with, was killed not long after that in an awful car accident that claimed the lives of both her and one of her friends. However, when January of the next year finally came around, a glimmer of hope finally came my way. Somehow I managed to get a night job driving a truck for Mid Cities Motor Freight in Saint Joseph, Missouri. I loved the job. It was local driving, home every day, and the money was great. I have no idea how I passed the drug screen, though, but somehow I did. It truly was a new lease on life this time, but I still wasn't out of the woods yet, not by a long shot; the worst was yet to come.

▽ So, just where did he get money for all the drugs & alcohol ??

2. You Reap What You Sow

whose she?

I stayed with Tammy for two more months and was desperately in need of rest. I needed mental and physical rest. I was exhausted in every way possible and knew I couldn't keep going the way I was if I were to continue driving a truck. I thought if I could just get two paychecks, I could get a place of my own and separate myself from my old friends and maybe get on the right track and turn my life around. However, it would not be that easy.

In February 1997, Tammy and I got into an ugly fight and I moved out. At that time, all I had to my name was a suitcase full of clothes and an old car. I didn't know where I was going or where I would stay, but I knew I had to go. I called an old acquaintance of mine in Kansas City, the only person I knew who would even talk to me at the time. I asked if I could stay with him for a couple weeks until I got on my feet. He said sure, but the only problem was, there was a twenty-four-hour-a-day meth operation going on at his house, and a lot of strange people coming and going, so he couldn't guarantee how safe it would be if I came around. I knew it was risky, but I needed a place to lay my head and get some rest, and, furthermore, it was only for a few days until I could accumulate enough money to get my own place. However, I stayed there for a total of one week, and it was, without a doubt, the scariest week of my life. There were spaced-out, crazy people coming and going twenty-four hours a day, just as he said there would be. Guns, needles, you name it, it was all there. It was a living nightmare that would become hell on Earth before it was all over. I started to have weird thoughts of people raiding the house and killing everyone. I even heard a rumor that the local Kansas City mafia, or some related gang, was planning to raid the house and no one would be left alive. I believed something very bad was about to happen, and it would happen very soon. It was unimaginable stress that was far beyond what I could bear at the time.

Then on March 5, 1997, six days after my initial arrival, I left the house for work and had made up my mind that when I got off work the next morning, I would pack my suitcase and be gone. Again, I had no idea where I was going to go or where I would stay, but anywhere was better than there)I got off work early the next morning of March 6, 1997, and headed to North Kansas City, where I was staying. When I arrived, I thought I would just take a short nap, pack my suitcase, and get out while I still could.

As it turned out, though, it was already too late and my opportunity had already passed. Shortly after my conversion to Christianity the seeds for evangelism were planted when the Lord revealed to me that that is the fate of many well-intended people who keep ignoring the warning signs and putting off His window of time allotted to them for salvation. It is like the timeless proverbial warnings; the road to hell is paved with good intensions and; no good deed goes unpunished! They will be horrified and utterly devastated when they discover that time has run out and judgment has come, unexpected, and like a thief in the night, as prophesied in the Bible. Like those people, I, too, heard the inner voice of God saying; "Now is the acceptable time, Ellis, today is the day of your salvation, turn back to Me now while the door is still open." And like them, I procrastinated one day too long, ignored the warnings, and learned; It is a terrifying thing to fall into the hands of the living God (Hebrews 10:31)! I went to a back bedroom to try to get some sleep. Shortly thereafter, I heard what sounded like a huge explosion. It sounded like a bomb going off in the house. People were screaming and bodies were flying. Without a doubt, it was hell on Earth. It was a covert operation executed by the Kansas City SWAT team all decked out in full camouflage, gas masks, and semiautomatic weapons, which they would not hesitate to use if necessary. Billy clubs were flying with force, beating down thugs who tried to run or fight back. They completely destroyed the house and whoever tried to resist in a matter of seconds, hauling everyone in that house to jail. It was, without a doubt, the scariest day of my life, and to this day I'm still amazed that no one was killed.

The DEA (Drug Enforcement Agency) spent the rest of the day and part of the next week gathering evidence from the crime scene. The house had been under surveillance for months, and by all accounts they had an open-and-shut case with everything they needed to send everyone there up the river for many years. I knew there was no way out of this one. I was told it was a federal case that carried a mandatory sentence of fifteen years to life if convicted. I later discovered I was charged only by the state of Missouri, but the charge still carried a multiyear sentence if I was convicted. They had all the evidence they would ever need to do just that. They had chemicals, they had a lab, and they even had a small amount of meth, along with fingerprints and used needles with DNA and other evidence they had gathered from garbage cans in front of the house. Although they wouldn't find my DNA on any needles, the DEA knew I had been living in that house for the past several days, and by all estimations, my life truly was over this time!

They took us to one jail in North Kansas City to process us, then to another to house us and hold us until we were charged and either appeared before the judge or bonded out. My bail was set at $50,000, and I thought I would never see the light of day again. I don't remember how many steel doors were slammed behind me before I finally arrived at my cell, but it was several, maybe six or possibly seven. For some reason, though, they locked me in a cell by myself, and I was so grateful they did. The last thing I wanted was to be locked up in jail with a stranger I knew nothing about.

There are no words to describe the horror I felt that day; I had never been so sick or so afraid in all my life. At that point, as far as I was concerned, time had run out and my life was over. From what I had been told by the people who were supposed to know, I had absolutely no hope of ever getting out again. They had full intentions of putting us in prison for the rest of our lives if they could, and that's exactly what they set out to do. However, what happened next, on that unforgettable day, March 6, 1997, and then over the next two years and still today, defies all the natural laws of the known universe, or anywhere else for that matter.

I had a life-changing encounter that no judge, jury, or any other man-made establishment could do anything about; not even the gates of hell or Satan himself could stop what happened next. It was the day that one life ended—and another began, the day Jesus Christ came into my life, revealed Himself, and rescued me from hell and eternal damnation! I can't tell you what time of day it was, as the entire day was fast and furious, so intense that I lost all track of time. It seemed like an eternity, though, just sitting in that jail cell thinking, "Who can help me now?" I remember sitting there for what seemed like hours on end racking my brain, trying to think of even one person who could help me.

The longer I thought about it, the more I began to realize there was absolutely no one anywhere who I could think of who would help me or, at that point, could help me, even if they wanted. That situation was far beyond the realm of human intervention. It would take a miracle of God to get me out of that mess! On top of that, the more I thought about things, the more I realized there was not a single human being that I could think of who even liked me anymore, let alone one who loved or cared enough for me to help me in that situation. I felt desperately alone and completely abandoned, scared without hope or even a single human being left anywhere on this Earth to turn to. Other than my mother, who had passed away, and a wife who left and would never be back, I couldn't think of a single person anywhere who still loved me. That was as poor as I've ever felt in my life. I was bankrupt spiritually, mentally, and physically! I was as far down in the gutter as you can go without actually dying and going to hell, which I felt may be coming next. It seemed like I was standing at the very doorway looking in.

However, at that moment, I heard a beautiful and comforting voice say, "Ellis, I love you! Remember Me?" I felt the comfort and presence of something or someone far greater than anything I had ever felt before. He then said, "Ellis, I have always loved you, but you have been running all your life. I am concerned for your situation and I'm here to help, and, Ellis, I am the only one who can help you now. You must choose today, life or death: choose life and live. I have so much I want to do in your life, and so much life I want to give to you if you will just trust in Me and believe. Ellis, I have a plan for your life!"

The first thing that went through my mind was, "I must be crazy." After all, I had experienced a lot of stress that day and I wasn't exactly playing with a full deck to start with, but now, I'm having a conversation with God. I had come to the conclusion that one of two things was happening: I was either having a true encounter with the true and living God of the universe, and everything my mother said about Him was true, or I was having an all-out mental breakdown, which I thought was probably more likely! With all things considered, it was just too much for my weary mind to process all in one day. However, what I did know and experience for sure was a sweet peace, comfort, and rest like no other time in my life, so much so that I really didn't care if I was crazy or not. Whatever happened was far better than anything I had ever experienced before, including cocaine, marijuana, or meth. I had absolutely no fear, and I was no longer concerned about where I was or what was happening. I was captivated by the moment, and I no longer had the feeling of being alone.

My reply was something like this "Lord, if that's you, I know you know everything about me. I know you know exactly where I am and why I'm here and where I'm going. I know you know all things. So, Lord, what kind of plan could you possibly have for my life now?" He said, "Ellis, if you will trust Me, you're not going to prison. I have other plans for your life, plans far beyond all you could think or imagine!" I didn't know what to think about all that. In my way of thinking, they had enough evidence to put an innocent person away for life, and there was nothing that could keep me from going to prison for the rest of mine.)

Shortly thereafter, I began to have a flood of childhood memories passing through my mind that was breaking my heart. I remembered the two small-town Baptist churches I attended as a very young child with my family and all the wonderful Christian people who loved me and shared the love of Jesus Christ with me when I was young. I thought how wonderful that seemed to me back then and how much I missed it. I remembered my Sunday school teachers and people like Marge Wharton and Jean Adams, who still bring a smile to my heart today, and a wonderful friend of our family, named Bill Noble, who I thought walked on water. I remembered my childhood pastor, Dick Lionberger, who tried so hard to shine the light and love of Jesus upon my troubled young heart during those early years, even going so far as to visit me in jail at yet another place and time in my life. Then I remembered my precious mother and how she used to say I would be a preacher one day and be greatly used by the Lord. That sounded so crazy to me back then, and in my wildest dreams I couldn't imagine something like that ever truly happening. But then I began to wonder how different my life might have been had I believed like my mother did.

What I mean is this: It wasn't that I didn't believe in Jesus, because I did. I always believed that Jesus was who the Bible said He was, at least to some extent, but demons also believe in Jesus and even tremble, but that doesn't change their eternal fate one bit, and I, too, believed, but because of numerous demonic strongholds in my life, I was in a similar situation as the demons. Ecclesiastes 3:11 says that God has set eternity in the hearts of every man so in that way we all have a built-in sense of wonder about God and eternity, and I truly believe that all professing unbelievers live their lives with a certain unrest and fear for their futures, as the following verse would indicate. *"He has made everything appropriate in its time. He has also set eternity in their heart, yet so that man will not find out the work which God has done from the beginning even to the end (Ecclesiastes 3:11)."* I would have loved to have been a born-again Christian and believed as those other people did. They were beautiful to me. But according to my twisted thinking, and for whatever reasons, I simply believed it was something beyond my reach and impossible for me to be! It wasn't who or what I was, or could be. In other words, I did not believe that I could be like those other people and live that kind of life. They were by nature good people, and I was just naturally bad. I thought I was destined to be that way and had absolutely no control over it. I tried to be good and even tried religion, but nothing ever changed inside of me, and the older I got the worse I became. I mean, seriously, if I could choose a beautiful life filled with peace, love, and abundant blessings, as opposed to a life that would land me in jail numerous times and wreak havoc in the lives of my kids and my family, I would choose the good life! Who wouldn't?

But that wasn't how things worked out for me. ▽ I couldn't change no matter how badly I wanted to or how hard I tried and, for that matter, I hated everything about me. It's a horrible place to be in one's mind, and to make things worse, I began to think about the mountain of problems I had that had plagued my life for years and the job I had started just two months earlier. I knew that drug bust would be headline news, and surely they would fire me the minute they found out I was there. In my mind, I had nothing left to live for, even if by some miracle of God I did get out of jail again. So I said, "Lord, even if you could get me out of here"—and at that particular moment, I somehow believed He could if He wanted to,— "I have nothing to go back to and no way to survive. I just started my job two months ago, and when they find out about this, Lord, they'll fire me for sure." He replied, "Ellis, not only will you not lose this job, you'll be number one at work if you trust Me!" I thought about that for a while and thought how it all sounded so good.

I mean, wow! Number one; how awesome would that be? I would no longer be the most despised and

▽ Because he _chose_ the wrong kind of life!

unwanted person on this Earth! But the truth was there was so much more wrong with my life that even that wasn't enough to change my heart. I had a mountain of troubles and a financial debt reaching higher than the heavens, and I couldn't bear the thought of them one more day. It would take a brand-new me and a brand-new life and then starting all over again from the beginning to fix my troubled life. I was far beyond all hope of any kind. As far as I was concerned, it was like the old nursery rhyme from my childhood: all the king's horses and all the king's men couldn't put my messed-up, broken-down life back together again. It was just too late for me at that point. You see, it wasn't just my job or the fact that I had just been arrested for manufacturing methamphetamine with intent to sell; I owed a debt to the IRS (Internal Revenue Service) to the tune of $41,000, a debt I could never repay no matter how badly I wanted to or how hard I tried. It was impossible! I had been running all those years and could not run another day.

I was tired, and my running days were over. I said, "Lord, it would be better to just go to prison and lose my life than fight this fight or live this life for even one more day; I just can't do it anymore!" Again He replied and said, "Ellis, I'll take care of the IRS." God assured me, with absolute certainty, He would take care of anything and everything I cried out to Him about that day. Nothing was too hard or even difficult for Him if I would just surrender my troubled life, with all my concerns, completely to Him that day and trust Him. He really did have a plan for my life. However, even after all those magnificent promises, it still wasn't enough to satisfy my weary soul. Looking back now, I think, "Wow, how great are the riches of God's amazing grace and patience toward those He loves, who will one day believe in Him? How far will He go to save a person's soul?" I simply couldn't imagine an all-loving, all-powerful, all-knowing, perfect God taking the time, or even having the mind, to love a wretched human being like me. I mean, seriously, I was in jail for goodness' sake. It's the last place on Earth anyone would ever want to be seen or found by the King of the universe, Jesus Christ! Not now, not ever! But you see, that's just the way God truly is. He is love, and nothing can separate us from the love of God that is in Christ Jesus. Not prison, nor guilt, not even shame or self-condemnation can ever separate us from the love of God, which is in Christ Jesus, and what He did next proves how much He loves not only me, but everyone, including you. I cried out one last time: "Lord, even if You could do all that for me, and Lord, I do believe that nothing is impossible with You, I have absolutely no one anywhere, anyhow, who still loves me."

My biggest concern, as I discovered in that moment in time, was an empty heart and a lack of love and intimacy. I had ruined every decent love relationship I'd ever had, and my heart was grieved from sorrow and regret. I was so alone, so broken and desperate for someone or something real to love, that all I could think was, "Lord, nothing else even matters anymore." I missed my mom and my wife so much I couldn't stand it anymore. I cried out with all my heart and said, "Lord help me!" He already knew what was on my mind before I ever said a word, and He said, "Ellis, I will restore all the love that was ever taken from your life, but you have to trust Me and love Me with all your heart, soul, mind, and strength. I want all of you! Part of you is not enough. You will have to trust Me completely, and then I will do it. I will make all things new in your life. Close your ears to the world and don't believe a word they say. They will think you're crazy and try to talk you out of everything I want to do in your life. Don't listen to anyone or anything that might weaken your faith. Keep your eyes and ears fixed on Me at all times, trust My words; walk according to My ways, and I will do it. I will forgive, restore, and heal your broken life."

3. Grace upon Grace upon Grace

He finally had my attention when He said the words "forgive," "restore," "heal," and "love." Still, my guilty heart wanted to know, "Why, Lord? Why would you do something like that for someone like me?" He simply replied, "Because I love you!"

At that very moment, my whole being started to crack and then shattered in a million pieces. All my pride, arrogance, and self-centeredness, everything that caused me to have a heart of stone, was shattered beyond repair. I could see for the first time ever what a poor, blind, miserable person I really was. I was a desperate sinner in need of a Savior, and unless I was "Born Again," I would never see the kingdom of God or my mother again. I said, "Lord, please forgive me. I need you, Jesus! I need you more than anything. I don't care who likes it or what it costs. Please come into my life, forgive my sins, and make me whole.

again." At that moment, Jesus Christ came into my heart, forgave my sin, and healed my life completely. He took away twenty-four years of drug and alcohol addictions as if they were never there in the first place. Not only did He take away the addictions that day, He healed me physically, as well. And please don't misunderstand me because God doesn't always heal people instantly like He did me that day. However, sometimes He does. I am the exception and not the rule.

For reasons I may never know in this life or the next, Jesus Christ transformed my life in a moment of time, filled me with His Holy Spirit, and made all things new, just as He said He would do. Then, over the next few years, and again, just as He said He would do, God fulfilled every promise He made to me that day, which I will share in detail further in this book.

First I want to share this beautiful passage from the Bible found in Psalm 107 that I thought so perfectly described my life's situation before I was saved and the relationship I have with my Lord and Savior Jesus Christ now:

"There were those who dwelt in darkness and in the shadow of death, prisoners in misery and chains, because they had rebelled against the words of God, and spurned the counsel of the Most High. Therefore, He humbled their heart with labor; they cried out to the Lord in their trouble; He saved them out of their distresses. He brought

them out of darkness and the shadow of death, and broke their bands apart. Let them give thanks to the LORD for His loving-kindness, and for His wonders to the sons of men! (Psalm 107:10–15).

Wow, how sweet is that?! I wonder how many people really believe the words in that beautiful Psalm—that for one thing, there really is a God who loves them and knows them with an intimate knowledge beyond all comprehension. There is a God who cares enough about them to save them from all their distress when they cry out to Him in their trouble with a sincere heart, even when their trouble is caused by their own sin, rebellion, and hatred toward Him. Well, in my case, that's exactly what it was. They were my troubles, caused by my sin and my rebellion, and my rejection of Him and the plan He had for my life from before time began.

I rejected Jesus from the start. You see, God didn't owe me anything and He never did, yet with a sacrificial love far beyond all comprehension, God gave his closest and dearest possession, His only begotten Son, that you and I might have a fair opportunity to be saved (John 3:16). In Isaiah 61:2–3 you will find the most beautiful expression anywhere of the heart of God, and why Jesus Christ stepped down out of heaven and entered this sin-infested world to give His life and suffer as He so willingly chose to do: "*To comfort those who mourn* [that includes you and me], *to console those who mourn in Zion* [the great nation of Israel], *to give beauty for ashes, the oil of joy for mourning, and the garment of praise for a spirit of heaviness, that they* [all true believers in Christ] *may be called trees of righteousness, the planting of the LORD, that He may be glorified (Isaiah 61:2–3)!*" Wow, how awesome is that? And as great as it all sounds, it's true and it's called "Grace", God's riches at Christ's expense. It's all for God's own glory and works in accordance with His eternal promise and plan for our lives. We just happen to be the beneficiaries of a life we could never earn and a life we most certainly do not deserve! So I say, *"Repent therefore and be converted, that our sins may be blotted out, then wonderful times of refreshing will come from the presence of the Lord (Acts 3:19)."* It's God's unmerited favor toward us, an undeserving people who fell well short of the glory of our all-loving, all-merciful God and Savior Jesus Christ.

I hope you never find yourself in a situation like mine, where all you have to offer God is a miserable life of shame, guilt, and remorse, before you discover the true breadth and length, height, and depth of His unfathomable love toward you, as well, but if you do, please know this, God loves you, turn to Him today. I hope you will know from reading this book that now is the acceptable time and today is the day of salvation.

Tomorrow's not promised to anyone! If God, who is perfect in every way, could love someone like me after all I've done and the people I've hurt, He can love anyone—especially you. Again, there are no human lives beyond God's infinite and passionate desire to love and to know, and no situation, pain, sin, or failure beyond His desire to forgive, heal, and restore. With God, all things are possible, and He has a plan for your lives, too; please don't let it pass you by!

The question is: do you truly believe what the Bible says is true? I once heard a story that went something like this: Imagine you were in a building and someone said there is a bomb inside the building and set to go off in ten minutes; everyone must evacuate immediately or die. If you truly believed there was a bomb placed inside the building ready to blow up in ten minutes, and that everyone in that building would die if they did not evacuate immediately, you would more than likely evacuate immediately. You would be pushing and shoving, running over anything and everything in your way to get out of there alive.

That's how true belief in God and faith works. It's a belief so powerful that it demands a radical change or action to occur in a person's life. What I'm saying is this: No one really wants to perish. No one in their right mind is likely to stay in a building that's about to blow up, unless for some reason they would prefer to die, and we all hope that would not be the case. It's the same thing with your belief about God, His Holy Word, and your eternity. If you truly believed the Bible to be the inspired and only infallible Word of God, that it is His Holy Logos, and that it is of supreme and final authority over your life, you would almost certainly shudder at the words written next, if you were not walking in a right relationship with Jesus Christ.

Now the works of the flesh are evident, which are adultery, fornication, uncleanness, lewdness, idolatry, sorcery [drug abuse], *hatred, contentions, jealousies, outbursts of wrath, selfish ambitions, dissensions, heresies, envy, murders, drunkenness, revelries, and the like; of which I tell you beforehand, just as I also told you in time past, that those who practice such things will not inherit the kingdom of God (Galatians 5:19–21).*

To put this all in perspective in relation to what I just said, no one really wants to perish, especially when it means they will be forever separated from God and family in a place called hell. I mean, just think about it, eons and eons and eons of centuries after centuries after centuries, without one second of letup, and not one second closer to the end of eternity. No way! No one really wants that, but that's what the Bible says will happen to those who refuse to comply with God's Holy Word in relation to their personal lives. So again

I ask: do you really believe what the Word of God says is true? Let me put it another way. If your religion hasn't changed your life, then you need to change your religion while you still can! *"Enter by the narrow gate; for wide is the gate and broad is the way that leads to destruction, and there are many who go in by it. Because narrow is the gate and difficult is the way which leads to life, and there are few who find it (Matthew 7:13–14)."*

Billy Graham once said, "Religion is like the flu shot. It will keep you from getting the real thing." Salvation can only come through a true, intimate, and personal love relationship with Jesus Christ. He is the way, truth, and life, and according to the Bible, there is no other way to the Father but through Him. There are absolutely no other common grounds or any other true religions, period, and friendship with the world is enmity with God. You can't have it both ways, friends; it just doesn't work. Sooner or later, we all have to choose: believe in Jesus Christ and by faith believe what the Bible says is true, or by default the choice is already made for us and it doesn't bode well in our favor. And the truth is we are here one minute and gone the next; our lives are like a vapor, which we all know is extremely brief.

It reminds me of when Peggi and I were living in Spearfish, South Dakota. Our organization did an evangelistic outreach at the Black Hills

State University called "Celebration Life Festival & Crusade." In Sturgis, South Dakota, which is approximately thirty miles from where the event took place, and where the famous motorcycle rally is held every year, there was a billboard on the side of the road with a crusade slogan that asked this question: "Smoking or non? How will you have eternity?" It may sound funny in one sense, and God does have a real sense of humor, but in reality it's a very real and serious question that we all have to answer at some point in our lives. So my question to you is this: "How will you have eternity?" I pray you too will make the right choice.

4. A New Beginning

Starting life over isn't easy, especially when you're thirty-five years old and don't know the first thing about what you're doing. I didn't know anything about being a Christian when I first got saved except for what I remembered from childhood. I imagine a lot of people can relate to that. To tell you the truth, I wasn't completely convinced that I really was a Christian for quite some time after March 6, 1997. I thought I was, but I needed some assurance.

However, just over four months later, God would make it perfectly clear what happened that day in the Clay County Jail. But just twenty hours after being arrested, I experienced the worst shock yet. I was sitting in my cell, still trying to get a hold on what had just happened over the last few hours of that day, when I heard an audible voice say, "Lucas, get your things, you're leaving."

It felt like a million needles shooting through every part of my body. I freaked completely. "Is that you, Lord?" I thought it was God talking to me in an audible voice and coming to take me away. I mean, He did say if I would trust Him, I would not be going to prison, and I believed what He said; however, I didn't think He would come and personally escort me out of jail that day. As it turned out, though, it wasn't God at all, but instead the front desk informing me I was going home. I didn't know it at the time, but they had intercoms in all the cells. Talk about crazy; the human mind is not designed to absorb that much shock in a twenty-hour period and still function correctly, and, to be honest, the thought of leaving that cell and the comfort of God's wonderful presence was not a pleasant thought at all to me at that point. I was filled with anxiety and found myself in a deep valley of doubt with a severe crisis of belief on my hands. I did not want to go. I was a weak and, even more, a very fragile vessel, to say the least, deeply afraid that maybe it was all just a silly dream and asking myself, "Was it really God in here with me or a figment of my cruel imagination?" I began to second-guess everything that had just happened, my whole born-again experience and everything else, including my miraculous healing.

At that point, the gates of hell were unleashing their fury inside my mind. I knew nothing about spiritual warfare, the attacks of Satan, or how to combat them, but they were flooding my mind like a roaring river. My mountaintop experience was brief, as Satan didn't waste any time before the evil testings began. He was there before I ever left the comfort of that cell, causing me to have mountains of doubt while wreaking havoc in my new life as a child of the living God. Satan knew God had an awesome future and an amazing plan for my life that would, in time, bring even more people into His marvelous kingdom, and I would soon learn that Satan would stop at nothing to keep that plan from happening.

He tried to ambush my mind with his famous one-line lie, "Did God really say that?" And, "You're a worthless drunk, and a filthy drug addict to boot. God doesn't really love you. And what makes you so sure you're a Christian now, anyway? You'd have to be crazy to think God would get you out of this mess, a broken and worthless wretch that's of absolutely no use whatsoever to Him. You are what you are, and nothing will ever change that!" For a moment I thought he was right, because that's how I saw myself at the time. And Satan's attacks were so intense I momentarily forgot everything God had convinced me of just moments earlier in the very cell where I was now being harassed. However, God would not leave me, nor would He forsake me when Satan came calling.

I soon remembered every word Jesus said to me that day. "Don't listen to anyone or anything that might weaken your faith." Well, that became my rule to either live by or die by. After all, if I were crazy, what did I have to lose? Nothing! Satan is, and has always been, a liar and a deceiver. So I made up my mind right then and there I would not believe another word he had to say, ever. I was standing on the promises of God that I believe were promised to me that day. "Keep your eyes and ears fixed on me at all times and I will do it; I will forgive, heal, and restore your broken life!"

I wanted that more than anything, including life, and nothing, and I do mean nothing, was ever going to talk me out of it again. I made up my mind to do exactly as Jesus instructed me to do, keeping my eyes and ears fixed on Him at all times and never, ever looking back again! I learned to resist Satan's wicked temptations by simply replying, "That's not what God said!" I would find myself repeating that very same statement over and over and over again over the next few months of my life. And like Isaiah, the prophet of old, I had this attitude in me: *"Because the Lord God helps me, I will not be dismayed; therefore, I have set my face like flint to do his will, and I know that I will triumph (Isaiah 50:7 TLB)."* I would not be moved again! *"There is now no condemnation for those who are in Christ Jesus (Romans 8:1)."*

The Apostle Paul recorded his understanding of spiritual warfare in Ephesians 6:10–17, and it has served as a life preserver for many wounded Christian soldiers marching on into the battlefields of life. It has both protected and guided me through many difficult seasons of vicious battles in spiritual warfare throughout my Christian life and journey, and I have yet to experience a single time when God has failed me in any way, no matter how difficult or unbelievable the situation may have been. The most important lesson I have learned so far is: the more these promises have been put to the test, the stronger my faith in God has become!

"Finally, be strong in the Lord and in the strength of His might. Put on the full armor of God, so that you will be able to stand firm against the schemes of the devil. For our struggle is not against flesh and blood, but against the rulers, against the powers, against the world forces of this darkness, against the spiritual forces of wickedness in the heavenly places. Therefore, take up the full armor of God, so that you will be able to resist in the evil day, and having done everything, to stand firm. Stand firm, therefore, having girded your loins with Truth, and having put on the Breastplate of Righteousness, and having shod your feet with the preparation of the Gospel of Peace; in addition to all, taking up the shield of faith with which you will be able to extinguish all the flaming arrows of the evil one.

And take the helmet of salvation, and the sword of the Spirit, which is the Word of God (Ephesians 6:10–17)."

These are not easy instructions to follow or apply when temptations and testing come, but they are the truths that will set us free when applied in our time of need. Perfect love casts out all fear; it never fails, and neither does God's perfect Word. His precious promises freely given to all who will receive that will never change, fail, or disappoint anyone who will put their trust in Him and believe. It is the key that unlocks the mystery of God's unfathomable grace and power upon one's life, and I will just say this: if people would just believe, oh what a difference it would make in their lives! Unfortunately, though, fear and unbelief, the two most common enemies of our faith, almost always win, robbing people of their miraculous, and even more, life-changing blessings, preventing them from experiencing the full extent of all God desires to accomplish in their lives. God wants to come to our rescue when we're desperate, exhausted, and hurting, when all hope is gone, and give us a new beginning and an abundant life, which none of us deserve. However, we must first believe that God does exist, and that He (God) and He alone is the rewarder of those who diligently seek Him (Hebrews 11:6).

You see, what you do and how you live your life will ultimately declare exactly what you believe about God, the Bible, and eternal life. Either you will trust God and live, or you will never really live life at all, but instead merely exist in a cosmos created for extraordinary life with a promised victory that truly does overcome this fallen world and all its disappointments and never experience the amazing joy of God's divine providence at work on your behalf, preparing a table for you in the presence of your enemies, and showing Himself strong on your behalf! *"The eyes of the Lord run to and fro throughout the whole earth to show Himself strong on behalf of those whose hearts are loyal to Him (2 Chronicles 16:9)."*

After reading the story of Noah and his family, I kind of feel like I know a little about how he may have felt at different times throughout his life. He spent 120 years building an ark when it had never rained before, not even once. Then, if that wasn't bad enough, he preached a coming judgment upon the entire world in the way of a worldwide catastrophic flood caused by— what else?—rain (Genesis 2:5). No one believed Noah; they all thought he was mad. No one even knew what rain was, because until the flood came, it had never happened. The entire world thought Noah was a lunatic, completely out of his mind. He was without a doubt the laughingstock of the world. People would mock him, make fun of him, and laugh at him every chance they had, and there was not a single person on the planet, other than Noah and his family, who truly believed that God would really destroy the whole world and every living thing on it with a giant flood.

Imagine what it might have been like for Noah's three sons and their wives if there had been such a thing as a public school system back then. They probably would not have wanted to attend, and especially knowing the world would soon be destroyed anyway in the not-so-distant future. If it were me, I would have screamed at the very thought of going to school and begged Noah and his wife to keep me home to work on the ark, anything to avoid the public ridicule and all the senseless mocking and persecution that would have happened as a result of being Noah's child. Perhaps that was how it was, but then again, maybe not. The fact of the matter is, though, they were the only ones who were saved when the flood came, and here's why: Noah's family, though severely tested and tried, knew God, believed God, and then obeyed God, even when no one else would.

That's what real faith is all about and kind of how it was for me when I first came to faith in Christ. Anyone who had any real knowledge about my situation thought I, too, was crazy, just as Jesus said they would. Most of them, with the exception of a handful of God-appointed guardian angels, sent to help me through that rough stretch of my early Christian life, believed that with all the damning evidence in the hands of the DEA, I would soon be going to prison for most, if not all, of the rest of my natural life. Other than a dear brother in Christ named Rick Simbro and the Jones family in Saint Joseph, I was essentially all alone. Most people thought I must have had some kind of mental breakdown or something along those lines from the shock of being arrested on such serious criminal charges based on what I said I believed would come to pass in the coming months and years of my life as a result of my encounter with Jesus Christ.

In their defense, I want to point out that not all were trying to be malicious or mean-spirited toward me. Although some were, most simply thought I had taken a trip over the cuckoo's nest and was no longer in touch with the real world. Think about it for a moment, a few months earlier I was homeless and barely eating, then I'm arrested and charged with manufacturing methamphetamine with intent to sell. Then I tell numerous people I met Jesus Christ while sitting in jail and, figuratively speaking, He promised me the world. What were people supposed to think? I mean, these events that I said would happen in the coming months and years of my life and have since come to pass were in all actuality events on a Biblical scale in comparison to that of God parting the Red Sea for His chosen people of Israel to cross over on dry land, beyond the reach of their arch nemesis, the pharaoh of Egypt, and then destroy the entire Egyptian army behind them. The chances of all those things coming true in my life were about the same as they were when all that happened back then, zero. If not for the amazing grace and power of God, it would never have happened. I like what Victor Marx, founder and president of All Things Possible Ministries, said about his life in his book, *The Victor Marx Story*, that later became a featured film, "When impossible is the only way out!" That's what I'm talking about. Amen!

Now, I'm not Moses, and this isn't a script for *The Ten Commandments* movie, but God did exactly what He said He would do if I would just trust Him and believe. And just for the record, I want to point out that many of the very people who were mocking me back then are Christians today because of what God did moving forward in my life. No one calls me crazy anymore, except maybe my wife from time to time, who knows me best and loves me like no one's business and calls me all kinds of silly things just having her fun! And even she bows her heart at the feet of Jesus in total surrender and adoration and marvels at the amazing grace God has lavished upon my life. Both she and I, along with many others, give all the glory and credit where it rightfully be-longs, to Jesus Christ, who gave it all, proclaimed it all, and fulfilled it all in a poor wretched life like mine.

I love what Psalm 40 says about another poor wretched soul, named David, a man after God's own heart! *"I waited patiently for the Lord; and He inclined His ear to me, and heard my cry. He also brought me up out of a horrible pit, out of the miry clay, and set my feet upon a rock, and established my steps. He has put a new song in my mouth—Praise be to our God; Many will see it and fear, and will trust in the LORD (Psalm 40:1–3)."*

5. Crossing the Jordan

Now, if you're not familiar with the term "Crossing the Jordan," it will be of no real importance to you at all, at least not yet, anyhow. For me, it means everything. In Biblical typology, it's known as a foreshadowing of a greater reality that has to do with our born-again experience, our coming spiritual war, and then possessing our spiritual inheritance promised to all born again believers in Jesus Christ. In the Old Testament book of Exodus, God's people of Israel were slaves in Egypt, which again in typology would represent the New Testament world system, which we all live in today, that is always at war with God and His Biblical world system, good versus evil.

Living in Egypt at that particular time in world history would have been a brutal, cruel life for a Jewish person. It was a life subjected to bitter pain and suffering caused by 400 years of slave bondage to a

49

ruthless "Taskmaster" known as Pharaoh. Pharaoh in typology is a type of Satan, reigning and ruling with an iron fist over his world kingdom. And we all know how Satan feels about God's people; he hates us all with a passion. Why? Because we were created in God's own image and in His likeness. Satan also hates God, who in the beginning held him in high esteem as one of his highest-ranking angels. Somewhere along the line, though, sin entered into Satan's heart, and he esteemed himself even higher than the true eternal God who created him, causing him to fall, and fall hard, as a result of that sin.

It's called pride, and pride always comes before the fall! Then Satan, who was also called Lucifer, was cast out of heaven with a third of all the angles, who were deceived by Lucifer and chose to follow him under false pretenses to an absolute certain doom. Satan was then cast down to Earth, where he is called the god of this world. He hates everything we are and everything we represent in this world; not just what we represent now, but what we represent for all eternity as children of the living God. We represent everything he defrauded himself of and everything he will never have again, no matter how bad he wishes he could. I'm talking about life, love, and worship. It's about God's eternal blessing and heavenly bliss prepared beforehand and lavished on all who love, trust, and obey Him. It's a time of eternal adoration, where the saints of God gather together as one and cast their crowns at the feet of Jesus, praise and worship Him, and Him alone, for all eternity.

Imagine this, an eternal celebration taking place in a golden city as big as our moon called the "New Jerusalem," a holy city coming down out of heaven from God, and having the glory of God. Her brilliance is like a costly stone, as a stone of crystal-clear jasper. It is a beautiful image, to say the least, and I can hardly wait to see it. A great complement to the glory revealed in a vast and glorious universe, a conglomeration of brilliant stars, planets, and galaxies, all masterfully suspended in their place, and so vast that even NASA can't say for sure how big the universe really is. It's the glory and power of God revealed by the works of His very own hands and on display for the entire world to see and marvel at for all eternity!

Well, you can see how Satan could get excited about all that, but his problem back then, and still today, was that there is only one God and ruler of the universe, and that person is Jesus Christ, who will share His glory with no one, and that's exactly what happened; Satan wanted God's glory for himself. He exalted himself above God, at least in his own mind, and wanted to be God and rule the universe. He wanted to be the center and object of all universal power and worship but instead fell to the lowest

depths possible. He went from being blessed above
all the angels to cursed forever and damned to hell, a
place of eternal conscious existence forever separated
from God. A place described as a lake of fire that burns
with brimstone and sulfur forever without end, and
where the worm never dies, a reference to the torment
and suffering that waits. Satan's not happy, and until
the completion of God's eternal redemptive plan for
humanity and creation, he continues to run to and fro
throughout the Earth like a roaring lion, seeking whom
he may devour. His mission is to steal, kill, and destroy
anything and everything in his path, including, and
especially, us, the human race (John 10:10). In other
words, we are the target of his bitter revenge toward
God. He is the root cause of all pain, sin, suffering,
and bondage. Whether it's a forced slavery in Egypt
thousands of years ago or slave bondage to drug and
alcohol addiction in America or around the world
today, it makes no difference—you fill in the blank.
It's all brought on by our own disobedience when we
are tempted and carried away and enticed by our own
lust. Then when lust has conceived, it gives birth to
sin, and when sin is accomplished, it brings forth death
(James 1:14–15).

The only hope we have is to humble ourselves,
pray, and cry out to Jesus for forgiveness and deliverance, and then never to look back again no matter

what. *"'Then you will call upon Me and come and pray to Me, and I will listen to you. And you will seek Me and find Me, when you search for me with all your heart. And I will be found by you,' declares the LORD, 'and I will restore your fortunes and will gather you from all the nations and from all the places where I have driven you,' declares the LORD, 'and I will bring you back to the place from where I sent you into exile' (Jeremiah 29:12–14)."*

You see, it's God, and God alone, who has the power and means necessary to deliver an entire human civilization, or even a single individual like you or me, from the hands of the Taskmaster, and it's God alone who can regenerate a ruined life and turn it around for His own glory. And only God can give you or me a future and a hope!

Well, just to the north of Egypt was the land of Canaan, named after the grandson of Noah, the famous ark builder. Again, the land of Canaan in the Old Testament also has a spiritual application for the New Testament believer today. In typology, the land of Canaan, otherwise known as "the Promised Land," is symbolic of our New Testament "born again" experience that begins the moment we accept Jesus Christ as our personal Lord and Savior and are born again. That is the time and place where we cross the spiritual Jordan, symbolic of water baptism and our baptism into the family of God. It's the place where we cross beneath the water, which is symbolic of the death and burial of our old nature and past life, and then rise again on the other side, resurrected from the dead into our new life as a new creation in Jesus Christ. Wow!

I can tell you that for me it was an awesome experience. I knew I was free from drug and alcohol addiction, I was free from the fear of being alone, and then finally, after twenty-four years of slave bondage, I was free from Taskmaster Satan for good, never to be bound by him again. I can't help but get excited when I revisit those spiritual markers in my own Christian life and the power that set me free. I was ready the minute my feet hit the ground to begin my new journey as a born-again Christian and follower of Jesus Christ and ready to take possession of my "Promised Land."

You see, just as ancient Israel was miraculously delivered from the hand of the Taskmaster in Egypt (a type of Satan)—through a number of supernatural plagues, hailstorms and fires, insect (locust or grasshoppers) and frog invasions, turning the water to blood, and then finally the death of all the firstborn males of both man and livestock at the hands of God working through his servant Moses (a type of Jesus Christ, our deliverer)—we, too, are delivered by the same supernatural power sent forth from the same all-powerful, all-knowing God as a demonstration of His amazing love for all mankind. No matter who you are or what nationality you are, God loves all the children of the world, including you, no matter what your current situation in life may happen to be.

God also demonstrated His supreme power and authority over all principalities, powers, and ruling authorities of the world forces of this present dark age. You see, whenever people cry out to God with a sincere heart, willing to repent and turn from their sin with the help of His strength and His grace, Satan is no match for the power of Almighty God. However, please know and understand it's not by might or power of our own, but by His Holy Spirit and grace, that we are saved. *"For by grace you have been saved through faith, and that not of yourselves; it is the gift of God, not of works, lest anyone should boast. For we are His workmanship, created in Christ Jesus for good works, which God prepared beforehand that we should walk in them (Ephesians 2:8–10)."*

Ephesians 2:1 says "we were all dead in our sins and trespasses" prior to knowing Jesus Christ and the power of His resurrection, and guess what? Dead people don't do anything for themselves; they're dead. Seriously, how many funerals have you been to where the dead person arose from the coffin and delivered his or her own eulogy? My guess is, probably not too many. Why? Because when you're dead, you're dead, and that's just the way it is. That's how it is for an unsaved, unrepentant person. They can no more save themselves from hell and eternal damnation through their good works or good intensions than a dead person can rise again from the coffin and direct his or her own funeral service; it just simply has not happened, nor will it ever."

Fortunately for the repentant person, God had the heart and means to both redeem and resurrect even the dead. *"But God, being rich in mercy, because of His great love with which He loved us, even when we were dead in our transgressions, made us alive together with Christ (by grace you have been saved) and raised us up with Him, and seated us with Him in the heavenly places, in Christ Jesus, in order that in the ages to come He might show the surpassing riches of His grace in kindness toward us in Christ Jesus (Ephesians 2:4–7)."*

Again, I say wow! How great are the surpassing riches of God's unfathomable grace and kindness toward those He loves? We may never know the full extent of His love for us ever, not in this lifetime or the next. It's just too vast to wrap our hearts or minds around. Israel was the model expression of God's covenant love on display for the world to see, a love He so desires to freely give to the whole world and one day will. I'm talking about every tribe, every nation, and every tongue. When Israel was walking in obedience with Jehovah God, they experienced tremendous grace and favor from Him, like no other nation anywhere at any time period in world history. In fact, you might say they were literally the envy of the world, and still are today. Now, don't get me wrong, because life wasn't perfect by any stretch of the imagination for Israel, even when they were walking in obedience with God, and it won't be until Satan and company are eradicated from this world for good. However, even with all the sin, death, sickness, and disease going on around the world, Israel enjoyed abundant life like no other nation ever because of the covenant love relationship they enjoyed with Jehovah God.

The closest thing I can think of is possibly the United States of America when we were a God-fearing Christian nation and walking in obedience with God. Israel is also the model for New Testament believers to learn from and grow from today because, with a very similar model and in a similar way, Christians, too, enjoy a covenant love relationship with Jehovah God, Jesus Christ. We, too, are on display for the whole world to see. It's a love story written in blood on an old rugged cross over 2,000 years ago when Jesus Christ demonstrated His great love toward us by laying down His own life on Calvary's cross and dying a vicarious death in your place and mine, to make atonement for our sins. It is the greatest expression of love ever shown, and because of that great love, we, too, can experience tremendous grace and favor just like Israel has for centuries and maybe more.

From the moment we accept Jesus Christ as our personal Lord and Savior and are born again, as taught in the gospel of John chapter 3, we immediately enter into a binding covenant marital relationship with Jesus Himself as the Bride of Christ. From that moment on, we are entitled to all the unalienable rights written in the marriage contract for the Bride of Christ, which is all laid out in the Bible. From that moment on, Jesus said: *"Ask anything of the Father in My name and in accordance with His will, and it will be given (1 John 5:14–15)."* Or: *"Trust in the LORD, and do good; dwell in the land and feed on His faithfulness. Delight yourself also in the LORD, and He shall give you the desires of your heart. Commit your way to the LORD; trust also in Him, and He shall bring it to pass (Psalm 37:3–5)."*

Israel discovered the land of Canaan was indeed a beautiful land that offered hope, promise, and freedom for the Jewish nation, a fortified nation protected from unexpected enemy invasions by God's own hand. It was a place to erect their temple and offer their ceremonial sacrifices and offerings unto God. I think it's ironic that the walls around Jerusalem in the Old Testament represented the salvation of God's covenant people, and the gates represented their praises, and after all God did for them, and all He's done for everyone else, I think He's due some praise. Not only was Canaan a safe and peaceful place to live and raise their families, it was a land flowing with milk and honey, a fertile land with fruit so big that one man could not carry it out of the field by himself (Numbers 13). This would be quite a change from the bitter bondage they were accustomed to in Egypt. Every Jewish person dreamed of going back and one day living in the Promised Land where they would be free from forced slavery for good.

You see, God had made a covenant promise to Abraham, the founding father of the Hebrew nation, centuries before. It was also a promise to all true believers in the Jewish Messiah—the promise that one day the land of Canaan would be their promised inheritance in full for all eternity. Although that promise is now fulfilled in part, and modern Israel is one of the most prosperous nations per capita on the face of the Earth, it's nothing compared to the glory that waits when Jesus Christ returns to Earth at His second advent, when He sets up His kingdom here on this Earth and restores the land of Israel to the original borders of the Abrahamic covenant, and not just Israel, but all of creation, as well. It's a time that will usher in a 1,000-year millennial reign, where Jesus Christ restores this planet and the nation of Israel to its original Eden-like beauty and a time that I believe is coming very, very soon.

There are many parallels between ancient Israel and a New Testament Bible–believing Christian. For instance, it's a covenant relationship that requires faith and obedience to work, with an imparted righteousness that comes straight from the heart of God with a guaranteed promise that if we will humble ourselves and pray, seek God's face and turn from our wicked ways, God will hear from Heaven, forgive our sins, and heal our land (2 Chronicles 7:14). It's also a time when our faith will be tested and refined severely through the fires of affliction that will come upon our lives and prove exactly what we believe about God, His Word, and eternity as judgment begins with the household of God (1 Peter 4:17). Like Israel of old, we will all discover that it's one thing to make it to the banks of the mighty Jordan River, pass beneath the waters, and rise up on the other side and enter the Promised Land, and another thing altogether to possess our promised inheritance and then live our promised lives.

You see, crossing Jordan, or accepting Jesus Christ, is just the beginning. From that time on, and until the time that we either pass away in physical death or are taken with the Lord's bride, the raptured church, we have three things—faith, hope, and love— to get us through the countless toils, dangers, and snares that life will most certainly bring our way. The greatest of them all is, without a doubt, love! Cherish it with your whole life; you'll be glad you did.

6. *Against All Odds*

Getting back to my situation at the Clay County Jail and the events that followed will be a joy to write about in hopes that it might shine the light of God's hope into your life or a family members and strengthens your resolve and perspective about who God is in relation to you and your situation. I hope you will take the time to research the facts for yourself, because once you have the facts, even a child can understand that what happened in my life from March 6, 1997, and on is nothing short of a series of miracles sent forth from God as another demonstration of His amazing love for mankind. Also, I would like to point out that the grace God administered over the course of my Christian life was never intended to bring glory or attention to me at all, but instead is sent forth as proof-positive evidence that God is indeed alive and well and loves the most unsuspecting people. It proves that the gospel message recorded in the Bible is true. This book is meant to bring honor and glory to God and to offer hope and answers to other helpless, hopeless, and hurting people, that they, too, might put their trust in Christ and experience the life-changing love that results in eternal salvation, Amen.

It was the early morning of March 7, 1997, the day after the drug raid, when they released me, my acquaintance, and some girl whose name I can't even remember anymore from the Clay County Jail. It was a gloomy day, though, I do remember that. My dad was waiting in the lobby to pick me up and to take me home with him to the farm. It was a nerve-racking moment for me, and I wasn't exactly excited about seeing him. I didn't know what his reaction to everything would be, but I didn't expect it would be very good. However, to my surprise, he was not as angry as I was expecting, but instead seemed genuinely concerned for me. As I mentioned earlier, I didn't have the best relationship with my dad at the time, and this wouldn't help. I had caused him many stressful and costly moments throughout my many years of rebellion. As I mentioned briefly earlier in this book, I had been to jail numerous times before, and this time it was for far more serious charges than before. I wondered how much more of this kind of trouble he could take from me.

Also, earlier in this book, I said I couldn't think of a single person anywhere who I thought still loved me. Well, that was especially true about my dad. We had been at odds for well over twenty years, mostly due to all the trouble I had been in over the course of my life, and I truly believed he hated me. However, over the next few years of my life, I would discover just how wrong I had been about my father and a whole bunch of other things, as well. Eventually I came to understand that Dad had his own spiritual war going on that I knew nothing about. He was headed toward his own encounter with Jesus Christ that would end with yet another string of miracles preformed in his life that were just as amazing as the ones done in mine. "Like son, like father." I'm so grateful to God for how things turned out between Dad and me. For families that are at odds with each other, and all hope seems to be out the door, it will both bless you and encourage you to never give up, no matter how difficult your relationships may be, or how impossible a breakthrough may seem. Remember, with God all things are possible; just keep taking it to the Lord in prayer and believing because good things really do happen to those who wait upon the Lord. You'll be glad you did. Not only did God eventually work all things out between Dad and me, He healed them completely. Dad has become one of my absolute best friends in life, other than my wife, and of course Jesus, and I can't imagine living a single day without him.

To tell you the truth, I honestly can't remember what the hurt even felt like anymore; it's just not there. God took it all away and erased the memory from my mind for good. The story doesn't end here, though, with my dad and me; it, too, got much worse before it got better. Immediately following my release from jail, Dad drove me back to the house where the raid had taken place and dropped me off so I could gather up some clothes and a few personal belongings from the house before going home with him to the farm. After we gathered a few personal items, the three of us—me, my acquaintance, and the girl—went to a local restaurant to get some coffee and talk about everything that had just happened. To my surprise, I was the only one there who had not been interrogated by the police or the Drug Enforcement Agency. I never gave a statement to anyone. Looking back now, I see how God had protected me from anything and everything that might have incriminated me. I don't believe God ever had any plans of me doing time in the penitentiary, but instead, He was preparing the way for my salvation and calling me into a life of service to Him. After our coffee time was over, we all broke up and went our separate ways. I went home with my dad to his farm, and my acquaintance left with his dad, I don't know where the girl went and I would only see her briefly one or two more times at court.

I told Dad about my encounter with Jesus while in my jail cell and everything Jesus said He would do in the coming months and years of my life. At the time, he just looked at me with disdain, in disgust. In his opinion, and the opinion of everyone else, I was on my way to prison for a very long time to come. Somehow, though, I think that deep in Dad's heart, he wanted to believe that what I was saying would somehow turn out to be true. I mean, he didn't really want me to go to prison, but I'd have to admit, even a preacher would have a hard time believing my story. Again, Dad wasn't necessarily trying to rub salt in the wound, and, for the first time in I don't know how long, he was genuinely concerned for my well-being. He didn't want to see his only son sent away to prison for the next fifteen years to life; he'd just lost my mother to cancer not too long before that, and he didn't want to lose me, too, especially not like that. However, all the damning evidence pretty much insisted I was guilty and there would be no way out this time. It was times like that, that I had to fight with everything in me to keep believing in myself.

Then in the coming days, Dad began to notice that I was not looking for a fix. I had no urge to do drugs or get drunk. It bothered him to see that I was having no withdrawal symptoms at all, and not only that, I seemed to be in perfect health. He was puzzled, and I think he probably thought I was temporarily in shock and that anytime I would fall off the wagon and revert back to the old ways. Well, it never happened, but at one point I tried, it just never worked. I truly was delivered, and this time for good. But to tell you the truth, there were many times when I didn't know how long it would last. This was uncharted territory for me, and I had no prior training or crystal ball to look into to see where my future led. From that time on, all I had was my faith and my jail cell experience to carry me through the thorns and thickets that lay ahead. At times I was as puzzled as the rest; it took a long time and a few more visits from God for me to finally figure out and truly know that life as I had known it before was over, and this time for good.

I had given my life to the Lord, and He was not giving it back. However, I was about to encounter my first serious testings that would tear my world and my heart apart and cause me to question everything I believed as true. However, the Lord would graciously and faithfully put it all back together again, only this time it would be His way and not my own. After all, He is the Potter and I am the clay, hard-pressed on every side and afflicted in every way, but by no means destroyed. I had told the Lord, "I don't care what the cost; I want You." Well, that would all be put to the test, and very soon.

I was heading straight for the refiner's fire and would soon find out being a Christian isn't easy. At first I thought God was punishing me, but now I know that it was all for my own benefit to teach me His ways and show me His faithfulness. I love what David said about the afflictions of God in Psalm 119: *"Thou hast dealt well with Thy servant, O LORD, according to Thy Word. Teach me good discernment and knowledge, for I believe in Thy commandments. Before I was afflicted I went astray, but now I keep Thy Word. Thou are good and doest good; teach me Thy statutes. The arrogant have forged a lie against me; with all my heart I will observe Thy precepts. Their heart is covered with fat, but I delight in Thy law. It is good for me that I was afflicted, that I may learn Thy statutes. The law of Thy mouth is better to me than thousands of gold and silver pieces (Psalm 119:65–72)."*

And afflicted I was! Things were not good at the farm following my release from jail, and friction was brewing between Dad, me, and his wife, Eva, who was basically caught in the crossfire. Eva was Dad's second wife after my mother passed and was a wonderful Christian lady whom I still think the world of today, even though she and Dad's marriage ended in divorce not long after that. It was uncomfortable and awkward staying at the farm, all things considered. I had so many things to sort through in my life, and I had a long uphill journey ahead of me that would take me deep into the wilderness of my life in search of the Promised Land and the peace that Jesus told me about, the promised life He said would be mine.

As I said earlier, Dad had his own spiritual conflict going on that I knew nothing about at the time. His financial situation was deteriorating and his business was failing. Dad had a lot of things on his mind right then that were tearing him apart, and this wasn't helping. The straw that finally broke the camel's back was the day when two of Dad's largest machine shops were destroyed on the very same day. One was full of antique John Deere tractors, and the other an entire fleet of semi trucks Dad used for his business. The second caught fire and destroyed every truck he had, while the other shop's roof collapsed from too much snow and flattened his antique tractors. To make things worse, neither was insured, and by that time, it was all my dad could stand. So after a couple weeks of severe tension at the farm, Dad rented me a place in Saint Joseph, and I think we were all glad he did. The conflict between us was not yet over by a long shot, and we would have yet another very nasty, difficult run-in before it was.

What's so amazing to me now is, with all the trouble brewing between us, neither could see that God was working all around us that whole time. Even in the worst and most difficult circumstances, and thanks be to Him and all to His glory, He would one day bring it all to a head and mend those broken fences for good. Wow, I can't help but want to praise Him right now for what great things He has done in my life, especially just knowing how bad the situation really was between me and my dad, whom I love dearly and am so grateful to my heavenly Father for. Dad is an unbelievable blessing and source of strength for my life today, and I can honestly say that should it all end tomorrow and God were to take one of us home, neither one would have any regrets.

Well, the place Dad rented was an old, run-down trailer with a door that wouldn't lock in a run-down trailer park where no one wanted to live, but to me it was paradise. It was a place where I could finally stop, catch my breath, and take a break from it all. It was a place of indescribable rest and solace where I would one day very soon, while all alone there by myself, receive the baptism with God's Holy Spirit. It felt like I had been electrified with indescribable love, grace, and power from up high, and I would never be the same again. It was also the place where God solidified my Christian walk and began to turn all my sorrows into immeasurable joy. It was the beginning of an amazing victorious Christian life where God would enable me, through the strength of His might, to overcome this wicked world and all the evil influences that kept me bound and chained for so many years, and harming so many lives in the process.

However, when I first moved in, I didn't have any furniture, eating utensils, or even a coffee pot to make myself a cup of coffee. Money was very tight when I first moved in, with my legal situation and then keeping up with my new place and all the bills, and I didn't have a lot of extra money to buy too many things with. I owed my defense attorney $4,000 and promised to pay him $250 a month until it was paid. So the first thing I bought while living in my new place was a coffee pot, filters, and some coffee (ha, ha). It felt so good just having a coffee maker. Then my sister, Brenda, gave me an old couch, a chair, and an old bed with springs poking up through the mattress. I was so grateful to have it, though, and she was just as grateful to get rid of it. It was the first time any of my sisters had reached out to me in years; they had all pretty much written me off years before.

Eventually I would become friends with two groups of people who owned used furniture stores not far from where I lived, Atherton's Furniture and the Bargain Barn. They were all wonderful people who bent over backward to help me furnish my home, and after all these years, I still have some of the very same furniture that I bought from them. It serves as a constant reminder of the life God rescued me from and how fortunate I am to have Him in my life. Mitch Atherton and his girlfriend, Gina, even went to church with me once, and it was one of the most exciting and memorable moments of my life. Because of them, it was so much fun building my kingdom at that little trailer and seeing it all come together right before my eyes. To be honest with you, though, I discovered my heart really wasn't as much about building my own kingdom as it was about loving Jesus Christ, getting to know Him, and then learning as much about Him and His kingdom as I could.

I was radically on fire after receiving the baptism with God's Holy Spirit, and all I could think about day or night was my Savior Jesus Christ. I went to a Christian bookstore and bought a brand new hardcover NLT Bible that I thought was easy to understand, and I could not stop reading that Bible for anything. I was consumed with the word of God. Words and passages were jumping off the pages as God began to open my heart and then my eyes to address the numerous impossible obstacles that lay ahead in my life, and all the places where I had erred in the past. Never before at any time in my life had I experienced such intimacy. I was in love, and probably for the first time in my life. I wanted to know everything there was to know about

Jesus, the magnificent Jewish Messiah and Savior of the world.

The more I read, the more I began to realize and believe that everything Jesus told me in that jail cell could and would one day come true. Everything I read in that Bible was directly addressing the mountain of problems I was facing in my life, including my current job (which I never did lose), my impending legal battles, and more. Especially the love He promised would one day be mine. I could feel my faith growing and my life changing with every waking moment, and I knew something big was going to happen in my life, and soon.

For the first time ever in my life, I found myself passionately wanting to go to church. Never before did I want to go to church as a result of my own free will. As a child, I was forced to go by my mother, and I swore that when I was old enough and on my own, I would never go again. But there was something radically different about me. I knew I needed to go, and I wanted to go! The problem was I didn't know where to go, and I was afraid to go alone. Once again, God in His unsearchable wisdom and knowledge knew exactly what I needed and would eventually lead me to the green pastures and still waters of Calvary Chapel Saint Joseph and Pastor Jim Morgan, where I would finally begin to settle down and grow.

But first I would embark on a two-year journey that would take me through yet another wilderness experience going from church to church, where I would experience everything from a barking preacher and miracle healers, to health, wealth, and prosperity on demand. All I had to do was pour everything I had into the offering plate and then sit back and wait for my ship to come in. Well, after a couple of years, my ship was almost sunk. It breaks my heart to see what goes on behind so many pulpits in our country today, and all in the name of Jesus Christ, with absolutely no regard whatsoever for the true spiritual needs and concerns of the many sincere people being taken advantage of. It makes me sick to think about it. I have a good friend in Kansas City who always says, "It's a jungle out there, brother El; you have to be an animal to survive." Well, unfortunately, he's right; it is a jungle out there and even more so in many of the mainstream churches in America today. Then I discovered that in one particular church, I really wasn't welcome at all after they learned about my past. My kind need not apply. That particular church went from over 1,300 people attending Sunday morning services under the previous pastor to a handful of people under that particular administration. They ended up selling most of their church property before the pastor skipped town and moved to another state altogether. Then I was told by the wife of an elder in yet another church I visited, who knew nothing about my past, "Those crazy criminals all deserve to go straight to hell." She said, "I wish God would do us all a favor and rid the world of them all; we'd all be better off if He did." Seriously!

I mean I couldn't argue the fact that we do all deserve hell, but I couldn't see how she was any more deserving of heaven than the worst alcoholic, drug addict, or prison inmate, for that matter. *"For God so loved the world that He gave His only begotten Son, that whoever believes in Him should not perish but have everlasting life. For God did not send His Son into the world to condemn the world, but that the world through Him might be saved (John 3:16–17)."* Romans 3:23 says, *"All have sinned and fallen short of the glory of God."* And Romans 6:23 says, *"The wages of sin is death, but the free gift of God is eternal life in Christ Jesus our Lord."*

Well, one thing was for sure, I had a lot to learn about the Christian community, and everything else for that matter, and learning would prove to be a painful experience before it was all said and done. There were no easy answers, no shortcuts, and no quick fixes for the burdens that lay ahead in my future. My dad used to say when I was a kid, "Son, it's a hard row to hoe." Well, he couldn't have said it any better; it would indeed be a hard row to hoe, and for many more years to come. I discovered I was a very antisocial person who lacked the social skills and abilities to communicate and interact with most people. And not only that, I was also struggling with a severe case of paranoia from the years I spent hiding out in the dark underworld of the drug culture, and large crowds of people would scare me to death, and it would be years before I was strong enough to go to church by myself. It wasn't long before I became depressed and borderline suicidal from my lack of ability to fit in, and I wasn't sure I'd live to see a better day. On one hand, I was thrilled to have my own place and the freedom that came with it, and even more thrilled to have what I believed was a genuine relationship with God, but I felt isolated and desperately alone in my mind. I began to doubt God's sincerity toward me and thought He had abandoned me, leaving me to fight this battle alone. It was a desperate and dangerous place to be in my troubled mind.

That's when I decided to give an old friend, Rick Simbro, a call. He is a friend I grew up with in Stanberry, and he lived not far from the trailer park where I lived. Rick was someone I felt very close to in my younger days; however, I hadn't spoken to him for at least two years and didn't know if he would even want to talk to me anymore. The last account anyone had of me wasn't exactly good, but Rick had always been a sympathetic person with a kind heart and gentle spirit. I felt like he was someone I could talk to about my situation.

The problem was that in our younger days we were old party buddies, and I had made up my mind that I wanted nothing more to do with the party crowd, and I wasn't sure how to explain to him that I was now a Christian and a follower of Jesus Christ either. However, I was desperate for someone to talk to and to be friends with, so I made the call anyway. I truly believe that is the most critical point in a new believer's life, especially someone coming from a similar background as mine. Satan knows when we are at our weakest and most vulnerable place. Those are the places where many new believers stumble and never get back up, rendering them useless in God's kingdom service and never knowing the full extent of His purposed plan for their lives.

I believe it is so important for churches to equip their members to reach out and embrace all new believers immediately following their conversion, no matter what their past life may have been like, and make them feel welcome and appreciated within the body and family of Jesus Christ. Offer discipleship training to help them grow and, in many cases, heal from their past experiences. Think about it, what would Jesus do in that situation? He would love them as if they were the only person He ever created and would assure them that they were important enough to die for. That's what Jesus would do!

Well, I was at that particular junction where I felt weak, vulnerable, and desperate. I was desperate for anyone who would look beyond my past to see who I now was in Jesus. When you're at that weakest point, it's so easy to make a tragic mistake and stumble; and, had I made the wrong call, who knows where my life would be right now? Praise God for being there when I was ready to fall. Amen!

"And He said to me, 'My grace is sufficient for you, for My strength is made perfect in weakness.' Therefore most gladly I will rather boast in my infirmities, that the power of Christ may rest upon me (2 Corinthians 12:10)."

7. Forgetting Those Things That Are Behind

I called Rick and said, "Hey, Rick. It's Ellis. How are you doing? I know we haven't spoken for quite some time, but I am now living just down the road from you and, to tell you the truth, I could really use a friend to talk to." Rick is one of those guys who were never very critical toward people when they found themselves in some kind of trouble, and in the crowd we ran with, someone was always in some kind of trouble. To my delight he said it was great to hear from me and asked how I had been doing and what was on my mind.

I told him all about the drug bust and my whole jail cell experience, including my encounter with Jesus Christ, and that I was a little scared and worried about how things might turn out. I told him I had accepted Jesus into my heart and that I was a brand-new baby Christian. Then I told him that I really needed a friend who would go with me to church somewhere for a week or two or until I was comfortable enough to go on my own. Little did I know it would be two whole years before that would happen.

His reaction was priceless, as he said, "Are you serious?" He was shocked silly and for a moment he didn't say a thing. Then, very excitedly, he explained that he, too, had become a Christian two years earlier and had been praying that God would send him a Christian brother to help him stay strong in the Lord. He told me he felt like he had been on an island by himself and that this was an answer to his prayer. He knew other Christian men, but it wasn't the same as having a close brother to share everything with, and I was just what the doctor ordered. Then he started to laugh and he said, "I was praying that Jim Heyde would get saved and that the Lord would send him, but I guess you'll do!" We both laughed hysterically; it was so funny at the time, and we still laugh about it today. The good news is that God indeed answers our prayers; He just doesn't always answer them the way we think He should. With the sweep of one large brush, though, God fulfilled the needs of two of His hungry children at the very same time. Rick and I became inseparable for the next two years, as Jesus Christ began to eliminate the pursuing armies behind me one by one, just as He had done for Israel thousands of years before.

We witnessed firsthand the sheer strength and might of Jesus Christ at work in my life and Rick's in ways that most people don't even believe exist. It was a period so intense that at times I didn't know if I would even live through it. God unleashed so much power that, before my deliverance was complete, I would be on my face crying out to God for Him to stop. I experienced so much stress those first six months to a year following my conversion that my whole body broke out in hives from head to toe, so bad that the doctors couldn't do a thing for me other than fill me full of cortisone once a month to help slow the symptoms. I was in the Refiner's fire, and the only person who could help me was Jesus, and He would not let up until His mission for my life was complete and I was ready for His service. That year the Lord rewrote the life story of Ellis Lucas, and I began to metamorphose into another person altogether, Ellis Lucas, the born-again Christian, the person I am today. *"Therefore, if anyone is in Christ, he is a new creation; old things have passed away; behold, all things have become new (2 Corinthian 5:17)."*

When I got out of jail, I went straight to work. I acted as though nothing had ever happened and, believe it or not, not a single person said a word to me about a drug bust or anything even remotely related to one. To this day I don't know if they even knew I was there or not. It was indeed headline news, though, and was one of the largest drug busts in the history of the state of Missouri at that time, and I assumed everyone had heard something. However, I was never asked a single question about a drug bust in all the time I worked for the company, and I never once offered an explanation to anyone. Before you knew it, there were weeks, then months, then finally even years that had passed and not a single mention of March 6, 1997. And then over the next four years, I would climb to number fifteen on the seniority board with over thirty other drivers below me, and life was just getting started. Have a God-sized need, friends? Call upon the name of Jesus! *"Call to Me, and I will answer you, and show you great and mighty things, which you do not know (Jeremiah 33:3)."* Both Rick and I worked nights back then, so we had all the time in the world to get together every single day, and weekends too, to read our Bibles together and pray for sometimes hours on end. Every day we would pray that God would bring to pass everything I believed He said He would in the Clay County Jail, which He so faithfully did in the coming months and years of my life, just as He promised He would do.

At that time Rick worked for the US Post Office in downtown Saint Joseph, which was located on the second floor of a four-story building at Eighth Street and Edmond. It was a great job; Rick had been there for many years by that time and knew every person in the place. That particular place would turn out to be my equivalent to ancient Israel's Red Sea experience before it was all said and done. That was the place where they were backed up to the water's edge with the Egyptian army in hot pursuit behind them. Their only options were to take God at His Word, trust Him, and cross the great Red Sea or give up, stay there, and die. God would either do what Moses said He would do, or their lives were finished. They had no other choice but to trust God and keep moving forward as He instructed them to do, or surrender their lives to Pharaoh and die. Well that's exactly how it was for me, too; I had nowhere to go but forward with God as He instructed me to do, or give up, go to prison, and take my chances there.

I was instructed to keep my eyes and ears fixed on Jesus at all times, trust Him with all my heart, soul, mind, and strength, and He would do it; He would forgive, heal, and restore my broken life. There would be no turning back if I was ever going to see God's Promised Land for my life. As you put the pieces of my life together, all true believers will see the fingerprints of God on everything, how He orchestrated my whole deliverance and healing from start to finish, just as He did for ancient Israel all those years ago. For so many people who knew me before I was saved,

God has used my life and testimony as a lightning rod to attract them to Himself, to offer hope, healing, and a new beginning to them, as well. The world of unbelievers could never comprehend how all this happened, and the truth is they never will without God's help and their cooperation with Him. There is none so blind as those who absolutely refuse to open their own hearts and minds to see. *"But the natural man does not receive the things of the Spirit of God, for they are foolishness to him; nor can he know them, because they are spiritually discerned. (1 Corinthians 2:1)."*

"For it is written: 'I will destroy the wisdom of the wise, and bring to nothing the understanding of the prudent.' Where is the wise? Where is the scribe? Where is the disputer of this age? Has not God made foolish the wisdom of this world? For since, in the wisdom of God, the world through wisdom did not know God. It pleased God through the foolishness of the message preached to save those who believe (1 Corinthians 1:19–21)."

I would indeed see the power of God's mighty hand to save, but also His tender heart where His mercies were new every day to sustain and uphold a broken and fragile life during the time I spent at the mercy of the Clay County judicial system. Almost every month I would show up for my court appearance to appear before the judge and plead my case, and every month I would hear the same old story: "Your hearing is postponed for this reason or the other. You will have to come back again next month."

That went on for what seemed like an eternity, but then somewhere in the neighborhood of four and a half months after my conversion, my dad received a call from my defense attorney, asking us both to come to his office in Kansas City ASAP. Apparently something so significant had developed that he wouldn't talk about it over the phone and insisted we come to his office immediately to talk in person. When we arrived, there were several well-dressed men standing around an oval-shaped table with puzzled looks on their faces. My attorney asked us to have a seat and said he would try to explain what was going on. He wasn't completely clear himself at that time, but he said he believed they were dropping all charges against me. He said the information he had received was they couldn't find a single fingerprint of mine in that house, and other than my being present during the raid, there was not a crumb of evidence to link me to the crime. I thought, "Are you serious? I lived in that house for a week; my fingerprints would have been all over that house!" At that very moment, I heard that voice say, "Now do you believe?" My jaw hit the floor, and I felt like crawling beneath the table to hide. My heart was pounding and I could hardly breathe, but in my heart I said, "Yes, Lord, I believe." I was terrified and shaking in my boots. I had never heard of anything like that happening before. My attorney was expecting me to be exuberant, but he didn't know the whole story, all that had transpired between Jesus and me. My dad was completely shocked, as well, and of course relieved.

Neither of us was expecting to hear that. My attorney told me to show up for my next court appearance just in case he had it wrong, but he was pretty sure he had it right. Sure enough, at my final court appearance, I was stopped in the lobby of the courthouse and told that they had dropped all pending charges against me. My attorney said I was free to go and I would not need to come back again. Wow, talk about growing up in a hurry. To whom much is given, much is expected, and although I wasn't familiar with that verse yet, that was exactly how I felt. "God, what do you want from me?" I had never really respected or feared any authority to that extent before all this happened, but this was no ordinary authority, and these were no ordinary circumstances.

I had pretty much been a free-spirited, carefree bum all my life before March 6, 1997, when all this began, but all of a sudden there was a very real and sobering sense of accountability to a much higher and far more lethal court than the one I had just been excused from moments before. I was instantly consumed by an overwhelming fear of God. You see, because of my complete lack of understanding of the true nature of God, I was not equipped to handle the greatness of His revelation in relation to me and my life. Although I was extremely grateful and very happy to not be going to prison, that particular experience nearly caused me to have an all-out breakdown right there on the spot.

I remember calling Rick that day, consumed with anxiety, and asking him to pray that God would help me make it through the day and that He would calm my troubled heart and weary mind, which Rick was more than happy to do. After that we began to spend even more time together, immersed deep in the Word of God like no other time before, praying for strength and understanding of these events unfolding in my life. Somewhere along the way, God gave me Philippians 4:6–7, which I memorized for my own peace of mind and spiritual well-being. *"Be anxious for nothing, but in everything by prayer and supplication, with thanksgiving, let your requests be made known to God; and the peace of God, which surpasses all understanding, will guard your hearts and minds through Christ Jesus."* There wasn't much time to enjoy my newfound freedom that eventually followed my dismissal from court and the pending charges against me. Satan was more determined than ever to destroy my life before anything else on the list had a chance to come true.

This testimony was for real now and, if it ever got told, who knows how many people would respond to the gospel and give their lives to Christ? He knew people couldn't just explain it away as coincidence, especially if anything else came to pass. He did not want to see that happen, and it wasn't long before I learned exactly where he would attack me next, my personal life and family relationships. However, before that attack would conclude, it, too, would backfire and add to an already exceptional testimony in Jesus Christ!

It all started when he managed to reignite the conflict between my dad and me. At the time all I had for transportation was an old pickup truck I borrowed from Dad when he first rented the little trailer house for me in Saint Joseph, as the transmission had gone out on my car. Dad had many vehicles to drive and at one time was considered a multimillionaire from a number of successful businesses he started from scratch. He didn't necessarily need another truck, except that this particular one belonged to my mother when she was alive. Mom would have had no objection to me using her truck at all, and for as long as needed, but Mom was gone. There was not a more generous and caring person on this planet than my mom. However, anyone who has ever dealt with Satan on a personal basis knows that he is the master of division and family breakups.

His favorite strategy is to divide and conquer, an ancient military tactic used throughout the ages where you divide and weaken your enemy, and then conquer them. It's as simple as that. And for whatever reasons, that truck would become the most divisive instrument on the planet, and my dad wanted it back. The problem was, until I was able to buy something to drive, it was the only way I had to get to and from work. The only credit I had was bad credit from old debts I had defaulted on in my BC days, or in other words, before I knew Jesus Christ. On top of that, the IRS had standing judgments against me with the power to seize any property I had, no matter who had an existing lean against it and without a court order, making it impossible for me to secure a loan for anything.

Once again, God would prove that no weapon formed against me would prosper (Isaiah 54:17); God Himself would see to that. Here's how it all got started. Not long after my dismissal from court, I rented another trailer in the same trailer park, only this one was on the other side of the park, which was like another world altogether. It was where the really nice trailer homes were. Not only did I rent one, it was a palace in comparison to the one my dad rented for me.

When Dad heard I had rented another place, he immediately got upset. He thought if I had enough money to rent a place like that, then I should have enough money to buy myself a car. Again, it had nothing to do with him needing the truck, because the minute he came and took it, he drove it straight to his weekend home on the other side of the state, parked it in his garage, and left it there for the next ten years. At that particular time, God was doing an amazing work in my life, like no other time before, and at the same time, Dad's was falling apart. Dad was the one who was angry and was on a collision course with his own God-appointed encounter with Jesus Christ. Dad had walked away from God years before to fulfill his own worldly desires for wealth and pretty much succeeded in his quest, but because God loved Dad so much, He refused to leave him to his own demise. But not before he came and repossessed Mom's truck and left me there afoot and on my own.

Well, down at the end of the street about a mile from my place was a used car lot with a gorgeous 1971 pearl-white short-bed Ford truck with a 289 V8 engine and a stepside short bed. It had been completely redone and looked awesome. Rick and I had stopped in there more than once so I could look at it and dream about it one day being mine. I knew that with my credit situation and the IRS judgments, I would never really be able to have that truck, at least not apart from another miracle of God. I would learn, though, that God's grace, like His mercy, is infinite and has no limits. Rick came driving up in front of my trailer that very day with $2,000 cash in his hand and said God told him to buy me that truck. Never before had I ever had a friend do anything like that for me. He said, "Hop in, bud. Let's go get your truck." Within two hours, that gorgeous little pickup truck was sitting out front of my home and the title was in my hand.

Once again I heard the words, "Do you trust me?" I thought, "Lord, how could you do this for me?" I knew I was so unworthy of that kind of love from anyone, and especially from Him! Dad and I didn't talk for a long time after that, and it would be years before we were back on good terms again. However, the following year would prove to be yet another miraculous chapter in the books and another "immovable" mountain moved on this magnificent journey of my life.

8. Facing the Giants

Not long after facing the giants of the Clay County judicial system, I found myself face-to-face with another breed of giants standing between me and my Promised Land, the dreadful Internal Revenue Service. But as fate would have it, they just happened to be located on the fourth floor of the very same building where Rick worked. After the dismissal of my court case, I was feeling pretty confident that everything else would simply fall right into place without a hitch. Well, you never want to assume that, as I would soon find out in the coming days. God continued to monitor my progress through the refining fires of affiliation to examine the depth of my faith and my overall trust in Him.

Rick and I had prayed for wisdom on how to deal with the IRS, and Rick had even discussed my situation with an IRS employee he was acquainted with who worked right there in the building. Rick insisted I go down and meet with them in person; he was sure something could be worked out on my behalf. One day I mustered up the courage and decided to gather up all those nasty letters I had collected over the years and head downtown to introduce myself and see what we could do to resolve the problem once and for all.

However, as I mentioned before, I was very much lacking in social communication skills, which at times got me into a lot of trouble saying the dumbest things imaginable; well, this was about to become one of those times. I gathered up my letters and headed downtown. I walked up to the counter, where a lady was working, asked if I could talk to her about a situation I had had for a number of years, and told her I wanted to know if she could help me resolve the problem. She said she would be happy to oblige and then asked me what the problem was. Well, it wasn't the easiest thing to explain, so I just threw my letters upon the counter and did my best to explain that I had gotten behind on my taxes in the amount of $41,000 and desperately wanted to resolve the problem for good. She asked how in the world I managed to get $41,000 in the hole. I explained that interest and penalties were more than the original debt and I had no way of paying the debt.

When I saw that that wasn't working, I began to share my experience from the Clay County Jail and how Jesus told me to trust Him and said that He would take care of this IRS debt for me. The look on her face was priceless, and to make a long story short, it went over like a lead balloon. She looked me straight in the eye and said: "You will pay every last cent that you owe and then some before this is all said and done!" Wow, I wasn't expecting that. I grabbed my letters from the counter and ran. I was terrified, and again it was all I could do just to breathe. The next day Rick came over to my place and said, "Ellis, I really believe you need to go back there tomorrow and talk to this other person I know."

He was sure that something could still be worked out if I just talked to the right people. He believed God was specifically directing him to tell me that and was convinced that I needed to both trust God and go back, or I would die in the wilderness of this life and with that nasty debt, much like ancient Israel did thousands of years ago. I told him there was no way I was going back there after that, but that night God pinned me to the carpet and said, "Ellis, you said you would trust Me no matter what. There is no turning back now. I can't help you when you won't trust Me. Be strong and courageous and I will do it; I will take care of the IRS!" At that moment, I understood there would be no turning back if I was ever going to see my Promised Land and be completely free from sin, debt, and bondage for good. The next day I told Rick I, too, was sure God wanted me to go back and try it again.

Rick assured me that this time I would not go alone, that he would go with me.

The next day Rick and I both headed to the offices of the IRS. Rick was right by my side. He walked me to the door, opened the door, said hello to the gentleman inside, then turned around, closed the door, and left me inside alone with the gentleman behind the desk. A lesson for you brand-new believers: He said he would go, and he did, but he never said a word about going inside. Always read the fine print. Rick knew this would be handled best in private, and he was right. I was so scared, though; and I could hardly even stand.

However, this very kind and gentle man saw I was having trouble and very calmly asked if I was all right. I told him I was not all right at all. He said he knew a little about my situation, asked me to have a seat at his desk, and assured me everything was fine. He was a wonderfully kind and gentle person with a beautiful spirit and calming personality and, in no time at all, I settled right down and we had a wonderful conversation. He said he had heard about my recent conversion to Christianity and said he, too, was a believer in and follower of Jesus Christ. He told me all about his church and family and the various ministries he was involved with. He was a wonderful person to talk to, and I soon began to forget all about my troubles in the midst of our conversation. As it turned out, we spent very little time talking about my IRS debt and almost thirty minutes talking about Jesus.

When he was finished with everything, he instructed me to file my taxes in the spring, and then every year that followed as I am supposed to do, and then not worry about this situation again. To tell you the truth, it took every bit of faith I had to go back after my first try, but one thing I've learned from walking with God over the years is: a faith that has not been tested is a faith that can't be trusted. *"The Lord is for me; I will not fear; What can man do to me (Psalm 118:6)?"* *"You are from God, little children, and have overcome them; because greater is He who is in you than he who is in the world (1 John 4:4)."* *"For whoever is born of God overcomes the world; and this is the victory that overcomes the world, even our faith (1 John 5:4)."*

I will have to admit I was glad when our visit was over and somewhat shocked that it all went as well as it did. I had such a liberating feeling of relief, knowing that something was finally being done to resolve the problem that had plagued my life for so many years, but the greatest feeling of all was just knowing that I was once again trusting God and walking by faith.

After our meeting I put it all in the Lord's hands and left for home, and when spring rolled around, I did exactly as I was instructed to do. I filed my taxes like any law-abiding citizen should do, and for the first time in over ten years, I was not afraid of the IRS. I was learning that if I truly trusted God and walked in obedience to Him that things had a funny way of always working together for my good. *"And we know that all things work together for good to those who love God, to those who are the called according to His purpose (Romans 8:28)."*

Life was finally looking up, and I felt the seasons of my life had finally started to change from a bitter-cold, stormy winter season to a beautiful springtime sunny day. My hives had finally gone away and I was starting to enjoy life more and more with each passing day, or at least until a few weeks after filing my taxes, when I got the shock of my life. I received a letter from the IRS, and inside was a check made out in my name for a little over $1,000. My heart stopped; I thought it must be a mistake. There was absolutely no way I should be getting money back from the IRS. The first thing I did was take it to my bank to see if it was real. Sure enough, it was a real check. I asked if it was mine or was it a mistake, and they said, "It has your name on it, so it's definitely yours." Well, I still wasn't convinced, so I took the check to the IRS and handed it to the same lady who rejected my plea for help the first time. She checked it out and said there was no mistake. I no longer owed the IRS anything and, as far as she could tell, the check was mine to keep.

Wow! If you haven't figured it out by now, God's love knows no bounds, it casts out all fear, and it never fails. Amen! But in order to walk on water, you must be willing to fix your eyes on Jesus, trust Him, and get out of the boat. If you will just give Jesus Christ a chance with your life, He'll prove His love for you is true! The Bible says God ordains our steps and delights in our way; He knows the end from the beginning and always has our best interest in mind and at heart. *"Trust in the LORD with all your heart, and lean not on your own understanding; in all your ways acknowledge Him, and He shall direct your paths. (Proverbs 3:5–6 NKJV)."*

I learned the statute of limitations had lapsed for collecting the debts, and according to our United States laws, unless it had been renewed by signing new documents during that time, it was off the books for good. Well, as it turns out, that's what happens when we accept Jesus Christ as our personal Lord and Savior. Your debt has already been paid on the cross at Calvary, and the moment we turn to Him in true repentance, our debts are forgiven and cast as far as the east is from the west, never to be remembered again (Psalm 103:12)! Satan's opportunity for collecting your sin debt is then over, and the Son, Jesus Christ, has set you free (John 8:36)! It took me a long time to figure out that what God had done for me was a gift etched out in love and paid for in full nearly two thousand years ago at Calvary's Cross, when Jesus gave His own life to settle your debts and mine for good.

What's so frustrating is we live in a society today where people are fascinated with all things supernatural, yet they reject the Lord Jesus Christ. We have ghost chasers, mediums, UFOs, you name it, and the list goes on and on. Hollywood is making fortunes on it. People spend millions of dollars year in and year out on fortune-tellers, psychics, and anything else they can find that will help them reach out and connect with the secret dimension of the supernatural.

Well, if it's the supernatural you really want, then open your hearts and ask Jesus Christ to come in. There is no greater power in the universe than Jesus Christ. If it's a miracle that you need, He is more than able and willing. However, there is no greater miracle that anyone could ever hope to experience than the miracle of a transformed life, a new beginning and the gift of eternal life and an eternal home in the New Jerusalem.

Many times I prayed and asked God to explain the mystery of the missing fingerprints and my situation with the Internal Revenue Service, and this is what I learned: *"Therefore, if anyone is in Christ, he is a new creation; old things have passed away; behold all things have become new (2 Corinthians 5:17)."* I am a new creation in Christ; therefore, there is no evidence to link me to the crimes related to March 6, 1997. Apparently, I went into that Liberty jail as one person but left as another. What I know for sure is this: there was no evidence to link me to the crimes that happened on or around March 6, 1997, so they dismissed all charges against me and let me go. You draw your own conclusion as to what you believe happened in my life on that particular day. As for me, I know exactly what happened that day: the old things passed away, and all things became brand new, exactly as the Bible predicted they would. As far as the IRS goes, this is what happened: apparently Jesus Christ, maker of heaven and maker of Earth, took it upon Himself to pay a debt He did not owe to erase a debt I could not pay. Amen! Again, you draw your own conclusion as to what you believe happened with the Internal Revenue Service, the fingerprints, or any of the events that are documented in this book. Was it a coincidence or a miracle of God? I'll let you decide. As for me, I know exactly what happened on this amazing journey in my life! It was, without a doubt, another amazing display of God's unimaginable mercy and grace for all eyes to see. Do you know what else? We still have a lot more to cover and a couple more promises to deal with before we're finished with the story about the Potter and the clay. "You'll be number one at work" and "I'll restore all the love that was taken from your life!"

9. A Season for Everything under Heaven

The book of James says if we see a brother or sister in need and do nothing to help them, our faith is dead (James 2:14–16). I learned a lot during that particular time in my life about the eternal attributes and true nature of Jesus Christ and about that particular portion of scripture, in general. Actually, there were two portions of scripture that were tearing me apart when I first got saved, one in the book of James, and the other in the book of Romans, where it talked about paying our taxes and setting a good example for our own conscious's sake (Romans 13:1–7). I felt so remorseful about my delinquent taxes that I found it difficult to even read that portion of scripture when I first got saved. I knew there was absolutely no way I could ever go back, pay all those taxes, and make things right again. I was barely making ends meet, living from paycheck to paycheck and keeping up with my legal fees and living expenses. Even though the Lord had graciously and completely pardoned my offense, I carried the guilt for years after my initial salvation. The thing that bothered me most was all the money I owed to various individuals from past debts I either defaulted on or just blew off all together.

So one day I sat down to make a list of every person I could think of whom I may have cheated out of money and made a decision that I would find every single one of them and not just pay what I remembered owing, but pay them back even more than I remembered owing, and that's exactly what I set out to do. I was so excited about doing it and could hardly wait to get started. I knew I could never repay the $41,000 to the IRS, but with God's help, the other debts I could.

What I discovered were two of the individuals I owed money to were deceased. However, their widows were still alive, and I learned they were both in dire straits financially and barely getting by. I didn't have the money to just start writing checks at will, so each week I would save everything I could to go toward paying these old, forgotten debts. The problem was I was afraid to go and approach them alone after all that time, and especially under those circumstances, so I called my oldest sister, Debbie, who I knew had been a Christian most of her life, to explain what I was trying to do and see if she had any advice or if there was anything she could do to help me. She knew these ladies well and said she would be happy to go with me to visit them.

I've never seen such shocked faces before in my life. They didn't know what to think when I told them how sorry I was and then asked for their forgiveness. Each one was more than happy to pardon my trespass against them. One particular gentleman, whom I owed several hundred dollars to, was so forgiving he wouldn't even let me repay the money I owed him. My cup was running over with joy, knowing each person was happy and even eager to offer their forgiveness and blessings on my life moving forward in Jesus. There was something so settling and satisfying about paying those old debts that eventually I was able to receive the Lord's pardon of the IRS with great joy, and after all these years even record those events that happened in hope that they may benefit those of you who may be dealing with a similar situation and say, "Thank you, Jesus," for my conscience is finally clear!

"How much more will the blood of Christ, who through the eternal Spirit offered himself without blemish to God, purify our conscience from dead works to serve the living God (Hebrews 9:14)."

Well, my conscience may have been clear, but I had a mountain of an uphill climb still ahead.

Holidays were especially difficult and very emotional times for me then, and I quickly discovered I could not make it through them alone. The first Thanksgiving and Christmas I spent at Rick's house with him and his family, who lavished their love on me every time I came around; their kids were especially awesome! However, when Easter rolled around the following spring, and I discovered I had no place to go, it was pure panic. Rick and his family were going to be out of town for the holiday, and I was plunged into a deep, dark, crippling depression, feeling isolated, alone, and scared. Before I was saved, my idea of a great holiday was getting together with the old party crowd and not even worrying about going home, because back then my heart was so hard I could care less about family and holidays. But now I was missing my family very much, and especially my mom; it was the loneliest year of my entire life. I never received a single invitation from anyone in my family for Easter dinner and, for that matter, I didn't know where they were even having our family get-together, if I did decide to try to go.

The pressure was building and my heart began to break. It all felt so hopeless that I started to come un-done all over again. However, I would soon learn that God knows my every weakness and would never aban-don me, but instead would abundantly supply for all my needs according to His almighty riches and glory by Jesus (Philippians 4:19).

By that time I had been blessed with another close friend, whom I worked with, named Kevin Jones. Kevin and I became very close friends after his wife left him and filed for divorce. Kevin never saw it coming and was devastated by the breakup. He knew from working with me that I was a Christian, and I was the first person he came to after their split. I felt so honored that he would do that. We talked about the whole ordeal, and my heart broke for Kevin. I knew exactly how he felt from my own experience. I shared the love of Jesus with him and told him all the great things God had done for me. I then prayed for him and asked if he would like to go to church with me the following Sunday. I thought if there were any relief or comfort to be had, he would have to look to the only true source for his answer, Jesus Christ.

I told him about my situation, how God had delivered me from numerous impossible circumstances, and how God, the Master Craftsman, whom Jeremiah the prophet refers to as the Potter (Jeremiah 18–19:13), was transforming and shaping my life into something beautiful, that God gives beauty for ashes. He listened to every word I said. After he heard my story, he said he would love to go to church and asked if I would pick him up so we could go together. Dur-

ing the invitation, Kevin went forward and invited
Jesus into his life and was now a brand-new born-
again Christian himself. It was an incredible experience for me to see someone I witnessed to walk to the
front of the church and surrender his life to Christ.
Kevin was the first person I had the joy of leading
to the Lord since becoming a Christian myself, and
I can tell you this much: you never forget something
like that. I began to see good coming from my past
mistakes, and through that experience my faith was
once again beginning to grow.

Soon after that, Kevin's whole family took me in
and more or less became my family and loved me as
one of their own. Soon they were all going to church,
and our little church family was also beginning to grow.
However, on that particular Easter Sunday when Caro-
line, who is Kevin's mom, heard that I was sitting at
home alone, broken in a million pieces, she jumped in
her car and came straight to my place and insisted I
spend Easter Sunday with them. She cried her eyes out
when she saw how bad I was hurting. I can't even begin
to express the love I have for that family or how grateful I am to God for bringing them into my life, and that
Easter would turn out to be one of my favorite, most
cherished memories of my entire Christian life. Caro-
line, if you ever read this book, I want you to know
you're the best, and I love you all very much! Thank

you for everything. You'll never know what a difference you've made in my life! That particular season of my life was one of the most painful of them all, and yet one of the greatest of them all for spiritual growth. I will remember it as the season of restoration, and not just from a lifetime of drug and alcohol addictions, a tragic and painful divorce, the loss of my mother, or a ridiculous debt to the IRS, but where God took hold of my heart, walked me through the valley of the shadow of death in the present dark age and deceptive world system and began the process of restoring all the years the locust and canker worms had eaten of my life! It was where my heart first began to heal and where all the love that was taken from me was in the early stages of a remarkable turnaround that would lead me straight into the loving arms of the most beautiful and caring person of them all, my precious wife and best friend, Peggi Sue. And although it would be ten more years before we met, I promise you this: it was worth every second I had to wait, and I would gladly do it all over again if it meant she and I would still meet, fall in love, and share this amazing life and journey together. So if you, too, are willing to trust God and wait for His best to unfold in your life, good things really do happen to those who wait upon the Lord!

Now, not only was my life supernaturally or miraculously well on the pathway to mending, I was about to witness yet another remarkable life-changing breakthrough, the long-awaited reconciliation with my dad. Remember the words of King Solomon in his assessment of life: *"To everything there is a season, a time for every purpose under heaven: a time to be born, and a time to die; a time to plant, and a time to pluck what is planted; a time to kill, and a time to heal; a time to break down, and a time to build up; a time to weep, and a time to laugh; a time to mourn, and a time to dance (Ecclesiastes 3:1–4 NKJV)."* Seasons come and seasons go; they will either leave you bitter or they can make you better. The choice is yours. I encourage you all to embrace them as God's blessed refining moments for your lives, knowing that He loves you with an everlasting love, and remember this: your greatest hopes and fulfilled heart's desires may be closer than you think, as it's always darkest just before the dawn! *"Weeping may last for the night, but a shout of joy comes in the morning (Psalm 30:5)."* Amen!

Speaking of the changing of the seasons, I worked four more years for Mid Cities Motor Freight after my release from jail, and, as I mentioned before, I had climbed to number fifteen on the seniority board toward the end of my four years. I had never held a job that long before, and things were really starting to look up. However, my sweet little pearl-white pickup truck that I was so proud of was showing the years of wear and tear and was in need of everything, and I just didn't have the resources to keep it up anymore. It was, however, one of the most precious gifts I had had in all my life and for good reason; it was a spiritual marker along my journey that marked the place where God stepped in and proved His faithfulness despite my lack of faith. *"If we are faithless, He remains faithful; He cannot deny Himself (2 Timothy 2:13)."*

Satan loves to pick God's weaker vessels apart by robbing them of their peace, their joy, and confidence with a continuous onslaught of trials, temptations, and testings that never seem to end. He keeps pouring on the pressure in hopes that we will one day fall apart and lose all confidence in our precious Lord and Savior for good. However, God's word seems to imply that Spiritual testing is created or allowed for our spiritual growth and future well-being, and that we should count them all as joy. *"My brethren, count it all joy when you fall into various trials, knowing that the testing of your faith produces patience. But let patience have its perfect work, that you may be perfect and complete, lacking nothing. If any of you lacks wisdom, let him ask of God, who gives to all liberally and without reproach, and it will be given to him (James 1:2–5)."*

How do you embrace spiritual conflict and temptation and count it all joy? Through prayer and the word of God! *"Do you not know? Have you not heard?*

The Everlasting God, the LORD, the creator of the ends of the earth does not become weary or tired. His understanding is inscrutable. He gives strength to the weary and to him who lacks might He increases power (Isaiah 40:28–29)." Well, I needed strength, help, and lots of power to overcome my current crisis of belief to attain a decent and dependable vehicle to drive. I was still in bondage to a bad credit history from before I knew Christ, which is a very difficult obstacle to overcome for anyone, and it would once again require God's divine intervention on my behalf to accomplish it.

I had started a bank account two years earlier at the Railway Credit Union there in Saint Joseph, where Mid Cities Motor Freight, the company I worked for, also did their company banking. The credit union just happened to be conveniently located in the very same building where Brother Rick worked. In fact, everything that was needed to rebuild my life just happened to be located right there in that very building, and Rick was the surgical instrument in God's hand. It doesn't take a brain surgeon to figure out it was not a coincidence. God had prepared the way well in advance with everything I would ever need to accomplish this remarkable restoration in order to accomplish His divine purpose for my life, and there was nothing Satan could do to stop Him or, for that matter, even slow Him down. It would all come to pass because of the many beautiful born-again Christian believers and godly relationships existing in that one building.

One of those beautiful people was a gentleman named Bill Harbison who worked at the Railway Credit Union. Bill was a wonderful Christian man who loved Jesus Christ with all his heart and has since gone home to be with the Lord and receive his eternal reward. Bill knew my testimony and was very sympathetic toward my situation. He truly wanted to see me overcome my past and go on to live this victorious Christian life in Jesus, which I am joyfully living out in all its fullness today. He would often offer his advice as to how to repair and establish a good credit history. The problem was many of those avenues were high-interest loans that would cost far more than they were even worth.

I knew that for me to get any kind of sensible loan, God would have to make a way. I couldn't imagine Him bringing me that far only to fail me. I just kept on believing that if I were patient, "God would make a way." Sure enough, one day while at the credit union, Bill took me aside and asked if I knew of a vehicle I could afford that would suit my needs. He said he would underwrite a loan for me through the credit union, and he would not require a cosigner for the loan. He knew the IRS debt had been settled from working in the building and that I had been with my job for over two years at that time. Furthermore, it was where my company did their banking, and my payments could be automatically deducted from my checking account weekly.

The very next week I did just that. I bought a 1997 Ford Ranger pickup, the same year that I was saved, with only 23,000 miles on it. It was like a brand-new vehicle, and it took care of all my transportation and credit issues for good. Once again, God had indeed made a way as He always does. What I learned later was that Bill had underwritten the loan as a personal favor to me on his last week at work before he retired from the professional world for good. It was almost like a presidential pardon, where a president pardons some undeserving person just before he leaves office. Because of Bill's kind heart, I was able to restore and maintain a good credit history for good. What I'm learning about God's grace, even after all these years, is we never get what we really deserve, which is eternal punishment forever separated from Him, and receiving those things we don't deserve, which is His unmerited favor an ever-lasting love. *"Blessed is he whose transgression is forgiven, whose sin is covered* [pardoned] *(Psalm 32:1)."*

God had provided an amazing future and hope for me, just as He promised He would do. The Bible says that Jesus came to give life, and that life more abundantly (John 10:10). Toward the end of my fourth year with Mid Cities Motor Freight, I was definitely living the abundant life, and for the first time ever, I was truly beginning to live the American dream. As for God, He was just getting started. I couldn't have imagined even in my wildest dreams the plans He still had in store for my life. I loved my job with Mid Cities Motor Freight so much that I started to think I might be there for the rest of my life.

Number fifteen was pretty good, and I really thought maybe that was what the Lord meant when He said I would be number one at work. However, I would soon learn that number one means number one. In the summer of 2000, while moving trailers at Weyerhaeuser in Saint Joseph, I saw a truck sitting in front of the building with a yellow cab, black fenders, and red wheels. It was filthy dirty and I thought at the time that it was the ugliest truck I had ever seen before. I remember thinking, "I could never drive something that ugly." The company's name was Estes Express Lines and they were based in Richmond, Virginia. I had never heard of them before, so when the driver came outside, I asked him who they were. He told me they had been around for over seventy years and were one of the oldest companies in America but were relatively new to Missouri. At that time their closest terminal was in Saint Louis, Missouri, which was over 300 miles away.

He told me they were driving all that way to take care of a wire account they had there in Saint

Joseph, but were in jeopardy of losing because of an interline arraignment they had with another company in the area that wasn't doing a very good job. Then he said they were talking about hiring a local driver in the area who would keep a truck in Saint Joseph and take care of the wire account. He asked me if I knew of any drivers who would be interested or if I myself was interested in something like that. I told him I was definitely not interested, but if he gave me a phone number, I would ask around. The guy's name was Jeff and, as it turned out, we would meet again. Jeff gave me the phone number, then jumped in his truck and headed down the road for Saint Louis.

I think my curiosity probably got the best of me but it was prompted by God's Holy Spirit, as meeting Jeff would turn out to be nothing short of a divine appointment from God. Just sitting here writing this book and remembering the whole string of events that followed that brief discussion with Jeff sends chills up and down my spine. I kept thinking, "What if this is some kind of dream job that pays twice as much as mine and all I have to do is walk out my front door each morning and, just like that, I'm at work?" After a few days I couldn't stand it anymore and I said to myself, "I've got to check this out and see what's really going on." So the next day I called the number, and a gentleman by the name of Steve Rogers answered the phone and asked how he could help me. I told him how Jeff and I had met at the Weyerhaeuser parking lot in Saint Joseph and that I was curious about the job he told me about. Steve said they had talked about hiring a driver in the area but at that time they weren't sure what they were going to do. He said if I wanted to give him my phone number, he would call me if something did come up. I gave him my number but pretty much wrote it off as something that I thought would never happen and eventually forgot all about it.

However, to my surprise, two months later I had a message on my answering machine at my apartment from a gentleman named Russ Jackson, who was with Estes Express Lines in Saint Louis, Missouri. He asked if I was still interested in working for their company, left his number, and asked me to give him a call. At that time I wasn't serious about changing jobs at all because, for one thing, I had no reason to change jobs. I was pretty much on easy street and basically in need of nothing. However, once again curiosity prompted by God's Holy Spirit got the best of me and I decided to give him a call. The next day I gave Russ a call, and he told me they were going to hire a local driver in the area and said if I was interested, they would come to my place in Saint Joseph and do the interview. That's when I realized they were serious.

He told me Estes had opened a dark terminal in Columbia, Missouri, and were gradually expanding their operation even further west. He said their immediate plan was to line-haul the freight to some meet point each day and exchange trailers with the driver from the previous day. I still wasn't serious about changing jobs, but I never told him that. Instead I asked him if I could just meet him in Columbia to look at their terminal and do the interview there. He said that was an even better idea that would work better for him. More than anything, I just thought it would be exciting to take a drive to Columbia and look the town over and check out some new scenery. However, on my way there, I asked the Lord if this was something he had worked out for my life, because I started to feel like there may be a major change coming in my very near future. I prayed earnestly and said to the Lord, "If I am supposed to change jobs, Lord, make it perfectly clear so I don't make a mistake."

It was just past my thirty-ninth birthday when Russ and I met in Columbia and did the interview. He asked about my experience and what my favorite pastime was. I thought that seemed a little odd, but perhaps he was just fishing around to see what kind of person I was away from work. It would be a huge

responsibility handing a complete stranger a set of
keys to one of their trucks and having him keep it at
his home 300 miles away. I told him I had been working
for Mid Cities Motor Freight for the past four years and
that my favorite pastime was learning to play praise
and worship music for my church. I told him I had
become a Christian almost four years earlier and that
I was hopelessly in love with Jesus Christ. I thought
that was one way of knowing if this was of God or not,
and it would confirm everything I needed to know. He
smiled a great big smile and said, "Wow, my family is a
gospel group that travels and sings." Then he said, "I
think you're the right man for the job." Before I even
had a chance to respond, he said, "We can give you a
truck to keep at home in Saint Joseph, and then we'll
meet in Concordia, Missouri, to exchange trailers each
morning." He told me how much they were willing
to pay me, which was almost twice as much as I was
making. After picking my jaw up off of the floor, I
asked, "How much did you say you were going to pay
me?" I wanted to be sure I heard him correctly.

The next thing after that, I was on my way back
to Saint Joseph to prepare to turn in a notice to Mid
Cities Motor Freight and start making plans and ar-
rangements to head to Saint Louis in January to start
my new job. At first it was very stressful getting used
to the idea that I would not be working for Mid Cities

Motor Freight any longer. It's always scary when you undertake a major change of that magnitude in your life, especially when I knew God had protected me and kept me there through the whole drug bust ordeal. The last thing I wanted to do was seem ungrateful to Him. However, if it was of God, I didn't want to miss out on a single blessing He had in store for me either. This was a classic example where the just shall walk by faith, and sure enough, God honored my faith.

On January 11, 2001, I caught a flight to Saint Louis, Missouri, to meet Russ Jackson and begin my new career with Estes Express Lines. Russ was a regional manager who oversaw the southwest region for Estes Express, but was actually carrying out the instructions of the person responsible for my hiring, a gentleman by the name of Mike Ingles. Mike was the right-hand man of Junior Johnson, the gentleman who called the shots nationwide for our company at that time and worked directly beneath our owner, Rob Estes.

It was truly an honor that seldom comes around in anyone's lifetime, and it humbled me to the core. Mike is someone that I am eternally grateful to and admire very much; he has been there for me all these years. I hope that one day he will read this book and see how God used him to fulfill a prophetic promise in my life, and even more, help fulfill the testimony that gave birth to the ministry of His Song Evangelistic Outreach Ministries, a 501c3 nonprofit organization based in Colorado, that I will cover later in this book.

But first there were a lot of things starting to happen that would alter the course of my life and the lives of others. I arrived in Saint Louis on January 11 and immediately began my orientation. I sat through two days of class work, learning all about delivery and pickup manifests, immersed in a ton of paperwork, before taking a safety course and a written test. Eventually, I was sent out with another driver for a road test. The first couple days were a whirlwind, trying to process everything I was learning and getting ready to leave out on my own. Then finally, after a few days of training, I was assigned a truck and a load and sent out on my way to Saint Joseph, Missouri. It was extremely scary at first because I had never had that much responsibility placed in my hands before, but there was no turning back. I made my first deliveries just fine, and to my surprise managed to get through the mountain of paperwork, too. The next morning Russ Jackson and one of the other managers met me at the meet place where I would exchange trailers with Jeff, the other driver who was on his way. After going over my paperwork and inspection book, they slapped me on the back, encouraged me to keep up the good work, and left. At that moment I was so proud to have that job and just praised God for the incredible opportunity He and Estes had entrusted to me.

I was overwhelmed with the feeling that something special was happening and I was exactly where God wanted me to be. I really enjoyed the guys who met me each morning at the meet place, and before I knew it, we were like family. There were three guys who traded off bringing my loads each day, and one of those guys was Jeff, the driver I met in the Weyerhaeuser parking lot. We became very good friends, and he would keep me abreast of all the latest developments with the company. Most of the time I never saw anyone other than those three drivers, but Jeff was the one who somehow always knew the inside scoop.

One day he asked if I knew about the buyout. I said, "What buyout?" He went on to say that Estes was buying GI Trucking, the interline company that had dropped the ball with the wire account in Saint Joseph, and the reason that I was employed with Estes Express Line in the first place. They were also the interline company that handled all our freight west of the Missouri line, but they were having serious financial troubles and were looking at possibly closing their doors. That, of course, would have created a difficult situation for everyone, including Rob Estes, and

the best solution was for Estes to purchase GI Trucking and merge the two into one company. None of us
drivers knew if the rumor was actually true until late
July 2001, when we were told that Estes had indeed
bought controlling interest in GI Trucking and that
we were to expect some major changes in the very
near future. Shortly thereafter, Mike Ingles called me
on my cell phone to say that they were moving me to
the Kansas City terminal in September and that he
would keep me abreast of the latest news. Then he
dropped the bombshell on me when he told me that
everyone who currently worked for GI Trucking in
Missouri, Kansas, Oklahoma, and Texas would no
longer have a job unless rehired as new employees of
Estes Express Lines.

Because I had eight months' time served with
the company, I would be the number one driver on the
Kansas City seniority board effective September 1,
2001. I was stunned and once again cried out to God,
"Lord, only you could have known this remarkable
turn of events." There is not an imagination anywhere
on the planet that could have dreamed this. Only an
all-knowing, all-loving God from eternity past could
have had the know-how and wisdom necessary to make
something of this magnitude come true. Mike set up
a time for us to meet at the Kansas City terminal in
August 2001 to introduce me to the terminal manager,

Mark Desorti, who took one look at me and said, "I think I can work with him." To my surprise, Mark, the terminal manager, was also a Christian. Mark and three other drivers soon became my best friends. The drivers were Jim McLeland, Dwayne Doyle, and John Smidl, all wonderful brothers in Jesus. We began to have regular times of prayer together at work and even visited each other's churches from time to time. It was truly a remarkable and blessed season of my life that I will never forget as long as I live! *"Every good thing bestowed and every perfect gift is from above, coming down from the Father of lights, with whom there is no variation, or shifting shadow. In the exercise of His will He brought us forth by the word of truth, so that we might be, as it were, the first fruits among His creatures (James 1:17–18)."* Amen!

10. Keeping the Faith

Estes wasn't the only remarkable thing going on right then; my spiritual life was thriving, as well. I was still a relatively new Christian, but I had really started to grow in my faith. Calvary Chapel was full of people with troubled pasts like mine, and after getting to know the people, I started to feel right at home. After being at the church for about six months, I was asked if I would serve as an usher for Sunday mornings. I wasn't sure what an usher even was, but I said yes and couldn't wait to get started. I knew there was a spiritual calling on my life from all the circumstances surrounding me and from a book given to me called *Harvest* by Chuck Smith. That book literally rescued me after a vicious satanic attack that nearly derailed me for good. I had gone through a devastating experience with another church that shunned me because of my past, and I was hurt so bad I began to think

God Himself hated me. I know it makes no sense after everything God did for me, but when the church rejects someone at such a critical stage in their Christian growth, it can be devastating. Israel felt that way when God brought them up from the land of Egypt and they were tested in the wilderness. They thought God hated them and had brought them out of the land of Egypt to punish, humiliate, and kill them there in the wilderness, and trust me, anyone who has been walking with God for very long has seen plenty of wilderness experiences and can probably sympathize with Israel's weakness, and mine.

About the same time when I was having the bad church experience, I was also serving in the prison ministry as a volunteer, where I led a young man doing two life sentences to the Lord. Shortly thereafter, I was barred from ever serving in Missouri prisons again because of something to do with my initial application and the screening process. Apparently, I had left something out on my application, and because of that I was barred for life. Those two events occurred within days of each other, devastated and nearly crippled my heart, causing all kinds of confusion and anxiety to accrue.

I soon discovered Satan had a new strategy on how to ruin my life; he would use the church as a weapon of war against me. When I first became a

Christian, I was very naïve, and Satan knew that the church could be a very effective weapon for an unprepared, inexperienced mind.

It may have even worked were it not for two amazing Bible teachers I came across on Christian radio while driving nights for Mid Cities Motor Freight. The two teachers were ministering serious healing through their messages, speaking directly to my battle-scarred heart and mind. It was as if they had lived my troubled life and were on the radio just for me. One was Pastor Raul Ries, the senior pastor of Calvary Chapel in Diamond Bar, California, and the other was Pastor Greg Laurie, the senior pastor of Harvest Christian Fellowship in Riverside, California. I had never heard of Calvary Chapel at that time and had absolutely no idea that there was a connection between the two teachers. Both of those pastors were written about in the *Harvest* book, which contains the personal testimonies of twelve individual Calvary Chapel pastors made up of everything from former gang members and drug addicts to mental patients and bikers, or otherwise known as society's rejects. They were people I could relate to in a very practical way, and after reading those twelve testimonies outlined in the book *Harvest*, I realized God was moving the world through the lives and ministries of guys very much like me.

I never questioned God's love for me again beyond that revelation.

The fact that I had never heard of Calvary Chapel is laughable now, because back then I had spent every Friday and Saturday night for the past several months in the basement of Calvary Chapel Saint Joseph, where the Olive Branch Coffee House was located. Rick introduced me to the Olive Branch Coffee House, which was the only place I felt comfortable hanging out. They had all kinds of Christian bands, and the atmosphere was very laid back and loving. Eventually I figured out there was a church going on upstairs, which turned out to be Calvary Chapel. I soon connected the dots and was able to set up a time to meet with the pastor and discuss my situation with him. He and I met for bagels and coffee and had an amazing conversation that turned my whole world right back around. He was extremely kind and understanding, and when I told him what happened with the other church, he said, "Ellis, your past will never keep you from serving God at Calvary Chapel." I cried like a baby after that and just thanked God for the *Harvest* book, the twelve testimonies, and for how He had directed my path to Calvary Chapel.

For the next three and a half years, I began to sense the call of the Lord on my life getting stronger and stronger, calling me to a ministry somewhere in the western part of the United States. I thought I would be living in Casper, Wyoming, and starting a church there, but God had other plans that would fulfill even the deepest hidden desires of my heart. But first I had another serious crisis of belief to deal with when one Sunday morning my pastor announced to the congregation he and his family were leaving the church for the mission fields on the Philippine islands. My heart was crushed, and I could not for the life of me imagine how I could move forward without my pastor's friendship, love, and guidance in my life. However, God was calling him to step down as pastor of Calvary Chapel Saint Joseph. I began to feel out of place all over again after that, and felt the Lord leading me to serve in another church. Then toward the later part of 2003, I received an invitation to join one of our former assistant pastors from Saint Joseph, Pastor Scott Gurwell, and his wife, Cindy, who had moved to Liberty, Missouri, to take over a struggling Bible study that eventually became Calvary Chapel Liberty.

The church was meeting in a bowling alley at that time, just blocks from the Clay County Jail where I swore up and down: "If I ever get out of this place, I will never come back again!" Well, apparently I was wrong. I would be going back to Liberty, Missouri, only this time not as a prisoner of the Clay County Correctional Facility, but as a bondservant of the Lord Jesus

Christ. When I first started attending church there, it was a bit of a shock going from over 400 people attending Sunday morning services to just over twenty people. However, it was great because we got to know each other much better, and I quickly fell in love with every one of them. I was finally able to take some Bible college courses that I had wanted to take for a long time through the Calvary Chapel extension campus that truly enriched my Biblical knowledge and understanding and lit an even greater fire in my heart for ministry.

Eventually I became the worship leader for our little church, and then one thing led to another until one Sunday morning while on my way to church I received a phone call from Pastor Scott saying he was sick and needed me to take his place and give the Sunday morning message. I was absolutely terrified but assured him not to worry, that everything would be fine. The minute I arrived at church, I rushed to the back room where I could be alone, opened up my Bible, and began to pray: "Lord, I've never preached before, and I don't even have a message prepared." He quickly reminded me of a class I had sat in on while at Saint Joseph called "Experiencing God," which was a twelve-week interactive class with a workbook and study guide. I started to reflect back on that course and, before I knew it, all kinds of things were coming to mind. I sat down and scribbled out some notes for myself, prayed my heart out to God, then preached my very first message. The most amazing thing was that I actually felt the Spirit of the Lord come upon me and empower me to preach that message, and it was awesome to experience God that way. I have to admit, though, I was glad when it was over and my nerves could finally settle down, and when it was, everyone was extremely supportive, knowing it was the first time I had ever done any public speaking of any kind. They were a very comforting and loving family, and I miss them all very much. The Bible says do not despise the days of small things or humble beginnings (Zechariah 4:10). I can't even begin to express my heartfelt love and emotions as I look back on the precious memories of those wonderful days in that tiny church in Liberty, Missouri.

11. Iron Sharpens Iron

Eventually our little fellowship finally began to grow until finally our chairs at the bowling alley were filling up with new people. One of those new people coming to the fellowship was a long-haired, wild-looking fellow by the name of Mark Webb. I remember the very first Sunday he came to church; he bent over the row of chairs in front of him to say good morning to the Pemburlin family and scared their young son, Daniel, half to death. Mark and I worked together at Estes Express Lines, and up until that time, it was at best a rocky and unpredictable relationship between us. For three years Mark had been a thorn in my side that wouldn't go away, no matter how bad I wished it would or hard I prayed it would. He despised and hated everything about me, and after three years, it started to become a mutual feeling.

Mark had grown up with an older brother who excelled at everything he did, including sports, dating, you name it. Mark despised his brother, feeling inferior to him in every way, and resented everything his brother stood for. Then when his brother got out of school and heard the call of the Lord to become a pastor and surrender his life to the work of the ministry, he didn't hesitate. Again, he excelled in his calling, which caused Mark to have a bad taste in his mouth toward all Christians, and he especially didn't care much for me. I was still a fairly new Christian myself, and boy did I ever have some growing and learning to do.

At that point, I couldn't understand why people would still hate me. I had been a Christian for a few years and had done everything in my power to live up to the name, but I still managed to get on the wrong side of some people. Mark and my dad were the worst and at one point at the top of my "cannot be saved" list. Those were the ones who had crossed the line and gone too far; there was no hope for them. Isn't it funny how quickly we forget our own pasts before God graciously reached out and pardoned us? Well, maybe I'm the only one who's ever done that, but I confess, I could not stand this individual, and I wanted him out of my life for good.

You see, Mark was a different kind of person who would come to work each day, hunt me down, and do anything and everything within his power to offend me

and persecute me. It was a game to him to see how far
he could push me, and he wanted more than anything
to see me stumble and lose my composure so he would
have a reason to blaspheme the Lord and mock His
holy word. For three years I managed to walk away
and never let him know he was getting under my skin.
I did everything I could think of to keep my walk con-
sistent before him as my mother had done for me for
a lifetime. Mark was one of those unique individuals
who had absolutely no fear of God whatsoever; he just
didn't care what he said or did. He was your classic
God-hating heathen who gloried in his foul behavior
and bad reputation. I had never run across anyone like
Mark before, and he was the most serious test of my
spiritual endurance to date. At one point he was so bad
that I began to pray, "God, we both know where he is
going, so what's the holdup? Why should I have to put
up with this?" Wow, did I ever have a lesson coming.

Mark ran the Maryville route, which was thirty
miles north of Saint Joseph and where I worked most
of the time. Saint Joseph had been my route since before we took over the Kansas City terminal, and Mark
went right through there every day. It was about the
same time that the movie *The Passion of the Christ*
first hit the theaters when Mark started stopping in
at the Woodstream warehouse, our biggest account in
Saint Joseph, to hunt me down to ask some very tough

questions that were on his mind. I didn't know it at the time, but some people had coerced Mark into watching the movie with them, and apparently it shook him up pretty good. He started hunting me down almost every day asking questions like "If your God is so great, loving, and good, why is all that violence and killing going on in Iraq and the Middle East? Why are all those women, children, and old people dying, and you're so-called 'Great God' won't do a thing to stop it?" I was a little shocked to learn he even cared that women and children were dying, and I wasn't quite sure what to make of all his questions.

He genuinely seemed concerned, and even a little worried, about the future of our world and the direction we were headed in. They were all legit questions, though, that quite frankly caught me somewhat off guard. This was not the same Mark that I had come to despise so much, and I found myself scrambling to find the right words to respond to his questions. However, I did my absolute best to answer him truthfully to the best of my knowledge and ability. I explained to him that there was an evil presence also at work in the world that you can't see but is real nevertheless, and his name is Satan. I told him that Satan was the one behind all the violence and killing, that God didn't have anything to do with it. He never could quite wrap his mind around what I was trying to tell him, and most of the time before I was through, he would jump up mad, make a mockery of everything, and then leave. He would always ask, "Why can't I be a Christian and still go to the bars and live the way I want to live? I thought God's love was unconditional." I did my best to explain that to be a Christian he had to repent and be willing to turn from his sins, with the Lord's help of course, and then live a new life in Christ. He began to stop in almost every day and argue with me about that, not wanting to give up the party dolls, wine, and the nightlife he loved so much. Then one day when he stopped in, I jokingly said, "Mark you can't straddle the fence with God. You have to choose—smoking or non, how will you have eternity? You can't have it both ways; you're either in or you're not!" I was trying to be funny, but he wasn't laughing. Instead he turned beet red, jumped in his truck, screamed a few curse words my way, and then drove off infuriated with me. I thought, "Where's his sense of humor? I thought that was hilarious!"

Around that same time, Jim and Dwayne, two of the drivers I had become close to at work, caught me in the parking lot one evening after work and told me they believed Mark was about to surrender his life to Jesus and that God had a special plan for Mark's life. They asked me to pray with them and intercede on Mark's behalf. They, John Smidl, and our boss, Mark

Desorti, had been praying for Mark for some time, and they genuinely believed that Mark would soon surrender his life in full to the Lord. I wanted to believe it in the worst way, but I was the one he hated the most and the one he took all his frustrations out on. I just simply could not picture it for anything.

However, I would soon experience the humbling of my own heart in a way that would change both my life and Mark's for good. It would alter the course of both our lives and drive us broken before the Lord on our knees, naked and ashamed as God exposed the true nature of both our carnal hearts and calloused minds. The Lord's chastening and stern discipline would stretch my understanding of the true heart and nature of Jesus Christ and show me just how much higher His thoughts and ways are than mine. And the truth is, I had become a narrow-minded jerk with a nasty judgmental heart of stone that resembled anything but the true heart and nature of my Lord and Savior Jesus, and the thought of it all still troubles me today. Mark was a test I had miserably failed as a representative of the kingdom of God that exposed the depths of my pride-filled heart and wicked mind.

"I counsel you to buy from Me gold refined in the fire, that you may be rich; and white garments. That you may be clothed, that the shame of your nakedness may not be revealed; and anoint your eyes, that you may see. As

many as I love, I rebuke and chasten. Therefore, be zeal-ous and repent (Revelation 3:18-19)."

The Bible says iron sharpens iron, a metaphor for man sharpening man, or making each other better men, or women for that matter. God makes us dependent upon each other, and He was deliberately using Mark Webb as a spiritual grinding wheel to grind off the rough, jagged edges around my heart in the same manner that iron would sharpen iron. It happens when there's lots of friction and the sparks begin to fly; at that point, something has to give. You're either going to come out a more rounded, more useful person, or you could find yourself a spiritual waste that usually gets thrown out with the trash. Your temperament is bad, leaving you of absolutely no use at all for kingdom work. However, I would soon see with my own eyes and experience with my own heart the truth about my own short falls and spiritual decay. It was the morning of April 18, 2004, that it all began, and just like any other morning, I awoke and opened my Bible to begin my quiet time with the Lord. I was reading from John chapter 12, which says, *"Whoever loves his life will lose it, and he who hates his life will find it. If anyone serves me, let him follow Me, and where I am, there My servant shall also be."*

After my devotion, I headed to Kansas City to do some business. However, my trip was interrupted by an all-familiar voice saying, "Go to Mark Webb's house and share the Gospel with him." My first thought was, "Get thee behind me, Satan!" However, deep in my heart, I knew it wasn't Satan. God was telling me that I needed to forget what I was doing and listen to Him. I eventually found Mark's house, but instead of knocking, I just took the liberty of letting myself in. I wasn't exactly excited about being there and wasn't planning on being there all that long anyway, just long enough to do what God had instructed me to do and then leave. However, I was about to get the shock of my life when I entered Mark's house. I opened the door and walked into a short hallway that led to the dining room at the end of the hall and to the right. When I turned the corner to the dining room, there was Mark, sitting at his dining room table with a Bible opened to John chapter 12. I thought, "Lord, what's this all about?" Mark's eyes got huge, and then he jumped up from his chair, ran around the table, threw his arms around me, and went to pieces. He was crying uncontrollably. Right then and there, God read me the riot act and said, "Don't ever think you know who can be saved and who can't ever again. Your eyes have become blind. I love this man, Mark, every bit as much as I do you, and he too has been set apart for My purpose!" I knew immediately how wrong I had been about Mark and that God was in that place. And where God is, there His servant shall also be. Mark was God's servant and belonged to Him. God really did have a plan for his life! Wow! I needed forgiveness, and not just from God, but also from Mark Webb.

Mark told me he hadn't been able to sleep for over two weeks and believed it was God who wouldn't let him sleep. He asked me what was happening and why God was harassing him. I told him I didn't know for sure, but I knew God loved him very much and I believed God had a plan for his life. He wanted to know what that meant and what he had to do. I told him he would need to surrender his life to God, trust Him, and obey whatever He instructed him to do. His response was, "I don't want to be a Christian." I told him that was between him and God; I was only the messenger sent there to tell him that God had sent His only begotten Son, Jesus Christ, to die on a cross to pay the penalty for his sins and mine and that if we believe with our hearts and confess with our mouths Jesus is Lord, our sins will be forgiven and our souls will be saved. Just before I left to try to deal with my own wretched heart, I said, "Mark, as soon as I leave, why don't you just bow your heart before the Lord, and say, 'Lord if You're real and You really do have a plan for my life, reveal Yourself to me, and I will follow you and do whatever you instruct me to do.'"

I'll never forget the next morning at work. I was already at work when I saw Mark walking across the parking lot near the front entrance to the terminal. I could literally see there was something different about him. It reminded me of the movie *The Ten Commandments* where Charlton Heston at the burning bush had a life-changing encounter with God, and then afterward his physical appearance looked different. It was the same way with Mark. I mean, he already had the gray hair, so it wasn't that, but it was his countenance and demeanor that stood out. You could tell by watching him walk across the parking lot that he was a born-again Christian. When he came through the door, he walked straight over to me, threw his arm around me, and cried like a baby. He told me and a whole room full of burley old truck drivers that God had shown him a vision of heaven and that he had given his life to Jesus Christ. From there he walked out on the dock and told everyone he saw that Jesus was real and that he had encountered Him the night before while alone at his house. From there he headed straight to the office of Mark Desorti, our terminal manager, and told him what had happened. The two of them bowed their heads and hearts in tears, cried out to Jesus, and said, "Thank you, Lord!"

The following Sunday Mark joined me at Calvary Chapel Liberty after a personal invitation from me.

That's where he began his own Christian journey, right there at that little fellowship in Liberty, Missouri. A few weeks later, we baptized Mark in the Smithville Lake not far from church, and when he came up from the water, he cried for the next three months straight. It was a very emotional day for everyone, and it reminded me of an old Gospel song the Oak Ridge Boys used to sing called "They Baptized Jesse Taylor in Cedar Creek Last Sunday, and This Time He Went Under for the Lord." I get chills just thinking about Mark coming up out of the water at Smithville Lake. Oh, what a day it was; thank you, Jesus!

"But I say to you who hear, love your enemies, do good to those who hate you, bless those who curse you, pray for those who mistreat you. Whoever hits you on the cheek, offer him the other also; and whoever takes away your coat, do not withhold your shirt from him either. Give to everyone who asks of you, and whoever takes away what is yours, do not demand it back. And just as you want people to treat you, treat them in the same way. And if you love (only) those who love you, what credit is that to you? For even sinners love those who love them. And if you do good to (only) those who do good to you, what credit is that to you? For even sinners do the same (Luke 6:27–33)."

12. Be Ready in Season and Out

That very same summer I got a call from a couple friends in Bedford, Iowa, asking if I could play guitar for a summer Bible study and cookout they were planning at their church. One of those friends was Steve Molson, another friend I had grown up partying with, from Stanberry, Missouri, and someone I never expected to see again after my salvation experience. But a little over three years after I was saved, I received a call from Steve while sitting on my couch at home in Saint Joseph.

He was reading from First Samuel, and I knew immediately he was saved. He cried as he told me how the Lord had rescued him from almost certain death, saved and restored his family, and gave them all a wonderful hope and future there in Bedford, Iowa. He told me how another friend, whom he worked with, had shared Jesus Christ with him at his lowest point, when he and Cindy were split up and ready to get a divorce. At that point his health was failing and his family was in shambles, yet somehow his friend was able to share the truth of Jesus Christ and His redemptive plan for humanity and lead him to the Lord. Soon after that, Cindy and all the kids were also excited about Jesus. It was a wonderful reunion for us because we were re-united on the right side of life, Christ and eternity. I was speechless when he first called; it was so great to see him for the first time as a Christian and brother in Christ. Wow, was he ever on fire for God; he practically lived at their church in Bedford, and he's lucky they didn't charge him rent for being there all the time (ha, ha).

When they asked if I would play guitar for their Bible study, I said excitedly absolutely yes and could hardly wait. At first it was just going to be a very small, intimate study where a small group of friends would reunite and fellowship for the first time since Steve and his family came to know Jesus. However, I had become very good friends with a gentleman by the name of Tom Barnett that I thought would be a great addition. Tom and I both played guitar and had originally met at an Assemblies of God church where we were both visiting on our quest to find permanent church homes for ourselves, and eventually we became very good friends. Tom also played bass guitar and was a very talented person. I asked him if he would be interested in going with me and playing his bass for the Bible study; he said he would be delighted to go but said, "Wouldn't it be great if we could find a drummer to go too?" Well, it just so happened I did know a drummer who might go, my friend John Smidl from Estes. John played drums on his church's worship team in Grandview, Missouri, and he, too, was a very talented guy. John said he would love to go. We got together the next week at John's house, and the next thing you know, we were having the time of our lives. For the next few weeks, we spent countless hours practicing in John's garage and Tom's living room, getting ready for the Bedford Bible study. By the time we actually did the event, we had a pastor coming to share a message and three other people to share personal testimonies, and over 120 people showed up for the event. That night the Spirit of the Lord came upon our little band, and we knew it was the beginning of something special. By night's end, we had been invited to travel all the way to Texas, by a gentleman who was in town visiting family, to play at a Christian music festival that took place every year there. We knew we couldn't go to Texas; however, we did agree to return to my hometown of Stanberry, where many of us were from, and play at the Stanberry community center located just off the downtown square. We ran an ad in the local newspaper inviting the whole community to attend, which was a bit of a stretch for me, and for good reason. At one point I had been completely run out of Stanberry, and the whole state of Missouri for that matter, because of all the trouble I had been in with the law in the past.

This was an enormous step of faith for me, as I had only been back to Stanberry briefly and only to visit family, but never long enough to cause any trouble or let it be known that I was even there. But now, enough time had passed that I wasn't all that worried about my old reputation anymore. I was a new creation in Christ and was actually quite excited about doing it. My whole reason for wanting to go back, though, was because everyone in the area, including my old friends, knew there had been a major change in my life, and most had heard about my conversion to Christianity. The biggest reason I wanted to go home, though, was to minister to my old party friends and lead as many of them to Jesus Christ as I could. Once again, I was in for another incredible shock of a lifetime. We rented the community center, set up our music equipment, and did everything we thought we needed to do to have yet another awesome hometown reunion with even more of our old party friends in the hope of bringing some much-needed and overdue hope into many of their lives, as well. We even cooked a whole bunch of food and set up several tables to accommodate the crowd we were expecting.

The night was scheduled to kick off at seven p.m. with a free meal for everyone, followed by a night of praise and worship and multiple personal testimonies, including those of Steve Molson and Rick Simbro, which proved to be a tremendous treat for the people of our hometown. I would lead worship for the evening, but I was so nervous I was almost sick. The later it got, the more nervous I became as I kept watching the clock to see what time it was. The closer it got to seven, the worse I became. It was about ten minutes to seven and not a single person had shown up yet. I was starting to feel dejected and felt embarrassed that we had even tried to do something like that. Then at five minutes to start time, I saw a single vehicle coming around the town square and pulling up in front of the community center with another not far behind it. Then the next thing I knew, the entire street on both sides was packed with vehicles and the building was full. There was not a single old friend from my past in the crowd, only farmers, businesspeople, and even my dad attending the event that night.

I was absolutely paralyzed with fear as we took the stage and I strapped on my guitar. But right then, I felt the presence of the Lord once again calm my fears and replace them with an indescribable anointing power from on high. I had never experienced the Lord quite like that before, and once we got things under way, I never saw a single person even go to the restroom until it was over. It was an awesome night, and when it was over, the people were crying, hugging us, and asking us to come back home and do it again. I was overwhelmed with emotion from the outpouring of love we received that night; it made a huge impact on my life that is still with me today, though I was disappointed that we weren't able to reach a single old friend for Christ.

The next morning, however, my dad called me and said he had been greatly impacted by the event. He had never seen me doing ministry before, and it shook him to the core. We began to talk a lot after that, and God was really starting to do a work in both of our hearts. Dad was so proud of what God was doing in my life, and for the first time since I was a little kid, he wasn't ashamed of me. Before that night, the town always looked upon me with disdain and disgust, and they never even mentioned my name to him, but now when they saw him in town, all they could say was how proud he must be of me now. God really was restoring my life, even in the eyes of the community that had once run me out of town, insisting I never come back. After that night, Tom, John, and I began to think of ourselves as a band. We loved to play and were somehow blessed with an ability to reach out and minister hope and healing to people wherever we went. Eventually we even began to feel a sense of calling from the Lord to do so. We were all involved with worship ministry at our churches, but Tom and I felt most alive when doing these evangelistic outreaches. Not to take anything away from leading worship at our churches, because we loved doing that also, but there was just something about being invited by a church and doing these kinds of events that made me feel so close to Jesus that just never happened anywhere else. Another good friend used to say, "I want to be so close to the heart of God I can hear His heartbeat." Well, that's how I feel when doing evangelistic outreach work. God was indeed doing a work in our lives and was using us now to put these small events together and share the gospel message for His glory.

We continued to explore all the possibilities as opportunities continued to present themselves and doors continued to open to us for even more evangelistic-type ministry, until eventually we decided it was time to name our little band. We flirted with the names *Still Waters Praise Band* and *Eastern Sky*, but after doing some research, we discovered there were many bands using those names. But then one summer day, while out running my Estes Express route, a thought came to me to call it *The Dry Bones Praise Band*, straight from Ezekiel 37–39. There was even a practical application and spiritual application for calling it that. We had all been dead in our sins and trespasses (Ephesians 2:5) prior to knowing Jesus Christ as our Lord and Savior, and like the dry bones in Ezekiel's day, we too would need to be spiritually resurrected into new life by the power of God in order to live again.

In no time at all I gave Tom a call to see what he thought. He loved it and immediately went to his computer to do a search; this time we were the only band that we could find that would be using that name. That name opened more doors for us than you could ever imagine. People either loved it or they hated it, and many people, surprisingly enough, had never even heard the term "the dry bones" before. One thing was for sure, it opened up many opportunities for us to share the good news of Jesus Christ. It was always fun to share where we got our name and also how God had resurrected Israel and brought them back into their own land after nearly 2,000 years of being dispersed to the four corners of the world. I marvel at the Lord's faithfulness to all His people. Eventually that name would become our band's identity, and it looked like we were settling in for a long and fruitful run in the evangelistic arena of ministry. However, after just a few short months together, John called it quits with *The Dry Bones Praise Band* to spend more time with his family and to better serve his church worship responsibilities. The time we spent together, though, was absolutely, without a doubt amazing and is some of my favorite memories of my early Christian years. After John stepped away from the band, Tom and I continued to stay very busy going from church to church, and the invites just kept coming our way. Sometimes it was just him and me doing acoustic sets for smaller churches, but other times it might be us and a few other musician friends we'd met along the way or maybe a special guest singer from time to time.

And then finally, after two years from the time we first went back to my hometown of Stanberry, we were making plans to go back for another hometown evangelistic outreach. This time we were doing the event outside at the city bandstand located in the downtown city park, and we had a special guest band, Alabaster, from Calvary Chapel Saint Joseph. We also had a special guest speaker, Mark Webb, who turned out to be quite an evangelistic speaker himself, leading countless individuals to Christ. There was a lot of thought and planning that went into that event, much more than any event before it. The planning was in part because (for the first time) I would be sharing a tell-all personal testimony of my life before Christ, openly and completely uncensored. Again, it was yet another attempt to reach out to our old friends in the hopes that it might open some hearts and eyes to see how much Jesus loves them also, and eventually we would get news that Jamie and his older brother Rodney Joe McMillan had also received Jesus as their personal Lord and Savior too, but that was some years after this hometown revival meeting. God bless you both!

It wouldn't be an easy thing to do, standing before my hometown trying to explain the thoughts and actions of a tormented young soul who caused so much pain in the lives of so many people. However, and for whatever reasons, I felt led to do it anyhow, and not just for old friends, because they pretty much knew my story already. But this time it would be for the people who didn't know. I have found that not everything I feel led to do makes sense to me at the time, but when it is of God, the rewards are unbelievable and often involve someone else coming to know Jesus Christ. Well, this would turn out to be one of those times.

Like the first event, we ran an ad in the local newspaper with a brief description of the outreach and who all would be coming and invited the whole town to be our guests. This time people didn't wait until the last minute to show up. They came early, pitching blankets and lawn chairs and filling up the city park. This time there were hundreds of people in attendance. It was a spectacular turnout. And I remember when the sun started to set and it was getting close to the time for me tell my story, I started getting nauseated, feeling sick at the thought of opening my heart up to who knows what, and I almost backed out. I remember telling Tom, "I don't think I can do it," but he said, "You can do it, and you need to do it, so let me pray for you."

We prayed, and then up the steps and onto the bandstand I went. I thanked everyone for coming out and then asked them to pray with me before I began. After that, and with the Lord's help, I began to pour out my heart and gave everything I had in telling my story, the story you are now reading yourself. People said you could have heard a pin drop while I was talking. Everyone wanted to know what had happened to cause such a promising young man with so much going for him to veer that far off the road of life and cause all that damage in the lives of so many innocent people, including my three kids. Well, it's not easy to explain a life like mine, but I remember praying as I was talking, "God, please give me words to say that will glorify You and help these wonderful people understand my tormented life before knowing You. Let them glean from my experiences in hopes that it may save even one person from making the same mistakes I did. Amen! When I was finished, the people were lined up to talk to me and share their own experiences, some even confessing their own past mistakes. But all shared their heartfelt appreciation to me for sharing my testimony with them. Even the banker and his wife were in tears, thanking God for what He had done in my life. Not one person criticized my message that night. After the crowd broke up, the rest of us joined hands and prayed that God would use that night to accomplish great things in the lives of the people who were there, not knowing if we would ever come back and do anything like that again, which as of the writing of this book, we have not done.

However, the very next day, very early in the morning, I heard my doorbell ring at my place in Smithville where I lived.

I jumped up and opened the door to see who it was; it was my dad standing outside my apartment door wanting to come inside and talk. This time he poured out his whole heart, saying that he had drifted so far from God and wanted to know what he needed to do to get his heart right with God again. Eventually we bowed our heads before the Lord and Dad asked God to pardon his sin and make him, too, whole again. It was truly one of, if not the most, remarkable moments of my entire life. We spent the next Thanksgiving and Christmas together, just he and I, and he continued to pour his heart out before the Lord and me, just wanting to find peace and forgiveness for his sins.

Dad was heavily burdened with guilt and desperately needed a touch from the Lord. I couldn't understand why he felt so bad, though, about many of the things he thought were so bad. What he was feeling guilty about wasn't even sin in comparison to the life I lived. Nevertheless, he needed to clear his conscience and make amends for the things he felt he had done wrong in order to find the true peace he was looking for. You can't imagine how proud I am of my dad, or how thankful I am to God for what He has done in both of our lives.

Today Dad is a transformed man in Jesus, and one of the most beautiful human beings I know. He is without a doubt one of the sweetest blessings and best friends I've ever had in all of my life! I know there are many families and damaged relationships in need of God's healing and restoration right now, and, "Lord, I lift up every single person and family in need of Your touch and pray for their complete restoration and healing as well and all for Your glory! Thank You, Lord, for what great things you have done in my life and for what great things You will be doing in the lives of so many people in need of Your comfort and love for their families as well! Let their celebrations in You begin! In Christ's precious name I ask these things! Amen!" *"So he got up and went to his father. But while he was still a long way off, his father saw him and was filled with compassion for him; he ran to his son, threw his arms around him and kissed him. The son said to him, 'Father, I have sinned against heaven and against you. I am no longer worthy to be called your son.' But the father said to his servants, 'Quick! Bring the best robe and put it on him. Put a ring on his finger and sandals on his feet. Bring the fattened calf and kill it. Let's have a feast and celebrate. For this son of mine was dead and is alive again; he was lost and is found.' So they began to celebrate (Luke 15:20-24)."*

13. Standing in the Gap

Well, I credit a lot of what happened in my dad's life and mine to what Mark Webb calls the Holy Ghost Mafia. This is a reference to three beautiful intercessory prayer warrior ladies, named Maxie Irwin, Madeline Hatfield, and Phyllis Combs, who, bless their kind and loving hearts, have all recently finished their race and have since gone home to be with Jesus. God had enlisted these three ladies to intercede on behalf of my biological family and me, as well as many other needy people. The reason Mark calls them the Holy Ghost Mafia is when they are called on to intercede on behalf of a spiritual conflict, they always prevail. I believe Satan trembles in their presence. Two of these wonderful ladies, Maxie and Phyllis, I had the joy and privilege of giving a ride to and from church every Sunday. We had plenty of time to talk and pray, which was something I always need plenty of. All three ladies had become very close friends to me and were an enormous support while I was serving as worship leader at Calvary Chapel Liberty. They prayed for me without ceasing, even calling me during the week sometimes just to see how I was doing and praying for me then. It was that outpouring of love from those three precious ladies that shaped the course for my life today. I believe they all knew how special their relationships were to me then, and still are today, especially after losing my own mother so soon. They restored a lot of whatever was missing due to my mom's early departure from this life, and I am eternally grateful to them all for being there for me when I needed them.

I especially needed their support in the spring of 2007 when exhaustion and fatigue began to set in. I became so tired during that time that I started to lose my voice and my strength from pure spiritual and physical exhaustion. My driving schedule kept steadily increasing at work until I was averaging nearly sixty hours a week; that included working Saturdays and sometimes even Sunday afternoons. I would finish my church responsibilities and then head straight to work and drive all afternoon. I was concerned that if things didn't slow down, I would have to step down from the ministry to save my job. I couldn't bear the thought of not serving the Lord and fulfilling His divine purpose for my life. It was my ultimate dream, and especially after my encounter in the Clay County Jail and all God had done for me up to that point. In fact, I wanted to be all I could possibly be for Jesus and tell the whole world about Him and what He had done in my life. The problem was, I served the Lord out of love, but drove a truck to make my living. I didn't want to quit the ministry, but I couldn't make a living at it either. It was a volunteer position, as the church could not afford a salary back then. I was between a rock and a hard place, and the only thing I knew to do was just try to hang on until the busyness passed and things finally began to slow down. I just kept on believing God would somehow make a way.

Well, the busyness never passed, and by midsummer I knew I couldn't hang on much longer. I was out of gas and running on fumes. Stepping down wasn't the only problem; I was the only worship leader the church had. There was no one to take my place. I was stressed out coming and going, agonizing day and night over what to do, and to be honest, I was scared. I was scared of losing my place with the Lord, whom I had come to love and adore so very much. I had never had a life so beautiful and rewarding before, and it felt like all my dreams were slipping through my fingertips.

The Lord had pressed upon my heart one day, while reading Acts 20:28 and serving as worship leader, that I was to keep watch over myself and all the flock of which the Holy Spirit (God, Himself) had made me overseer. And if that's what God made me, how could I possibly be forced to choose? I didn't want to quit, but for reasons beyond my control, it looked like my ministry days might be coming to an end. I had been hinting to Pastor Scott for some time that I was in trouble and didn't know how much longer I would be able to continue the way things were going.

I had never been that exhausted in all my life, and when September 2007 rolled around, I regretfully announced that I would be stepping down as worship leader at Calvary Chapel Liberty.

It was a very confusing time in the weeks following my decision to step down and especially for the congregation. Instead of me playing guitar and leading them in worship, I was sitting in the back row feeling alone and out of place while the congregation sang along with worship tapes and an empty stage. They couldn't understand why I could come to church but not lead worship. To tell you the truth, I was wondering the very same thing myself. It was a difficult time for everyone, but again, time would prove God's got the whole world in His hands, including my future and Calvary Chapel Liberty, Missouri!

Things got so confusing, though, that I finally came to terms with the fact that it was time for me to leave the church at Liberty. It felt just like it did before

I was saved; I didn't know where I would go or where I would stay, but nevertheless, I knew I had to go. I felt so lost at the time; I had settled in and been their worship leader for over two years—but now where would I go? After pleading my case before the Lord, I felt as though He was directing me to go back to Calvary Chapel Saint Joseph, where it all began, and stay there until I had further instructions. Looking back now, the whole situation reminds me of an old Garth Brooks song "Thank God for Unanswered Prayers." In reality I was just days away from the greatest breakthrough of my entire Christian life, but in ignorance, I was doing everything in my power to prevent it. Thank God His will was greater than my determination to stay and that He remained faithful to His plan despite my resistance. Instead of me sitting around depressed and feeling like a complete failure, I would soon be clothed in a beautiful garment of praise, thanking God for all those unanswered prayers.

The next week I stopped in at Calvary Chapel Saint Joseph on my route and talked to the pastor, who said I was always welcome there and that he was looking forward to seeing me. Well, for the first couple of weeks, I didn't go to church anywhere and wasn't sure if I would ever go again, but by the third week, the hounds of heaven were hot on my trail. I was desperate for fellowship and I had to go somewhere. Depression was setting in and I couldn't sit at home another Sunday. I had some very special friends in Saint Joseph who invited me to come and sit with them so I would feel more at home. So when Sunday came around, I hopped in my truck and headed to Saint Joseph for church.

My friend's wife was a complete nut and she was a riot to be around. She was always concerned about my personal life and for some reason always felt compelled to try to fix me up with her friends. Well, this day was no different, and as soon as I sat down and got comfortable, she elbowed me in the ribs, pointed toward a gorgeous girl across the aisle to my right, and asked, "What do you think of my friend Peggi?"

Peggi was stunning to look at, and when I looked at her, she turned and looked straight into my eyes as if she were looking straight into my soul, and once again I heard that familiar voice say, "She's the one I told you about, she will be your wife!" God said she was the girl he had set aside from eternity past to be my wife and help me in the ministry He had prepared for the two of us from before time began. He said she would follow me anywhere in this world He instructed us to go. Well, my heart has always had a hard time believing everything my mind tells it, and this without a doubt was definitely one of those times. God said He would restore all the love that was taken from me, but I never expected someone as special as her.

I hope all of you will know enough never to underestimate God's best for your lives. My expectations were set far too low, and when I saw Peggi, I wasn't even sure how to say hello to a girl like her. I had not mastered the art of social interaction, and I most certainly had not mastered the art of talking to beautiful, confident, and successful women. It may comfort you to know that when God does give us a beautiful gift like that, He doesn't take it back just because we're a little overwhelmed at first sight and can't handle it, or we never received a manual with instructions on how everything works. No way!

I believe God gets a kick out of seeing our reactions to His goodness, and if you think that beautiful gifts from God can overwhelm us now, imagine what it will be like when we see Jesus face-to-face and fix our eyes on the New Jerusalem! His ways are definitely not our ways. And trust me, when we wait upon the Lord, His best is far greater than anything we could ever imagine, and it pleases Him to be able to bless His beloved children. It is a living testimony to an unbelieving world that may draw them to Him in repentance one day as well. It has nothing to do with our social abilities, good looks, or anything to do with us, but everything to do with Him and how much He loves us and what Christ has already done on our behalf. It brings Him great glory when that happens, and as I said before, good things really do come to those who wait upon the Lord, and if we honor God with our lives, He will honor us in return!! "But now the Lord says: 'far be it from Me; for those who honor Me I will honor, and those who despise Me shall be lightly esteemed (1 Samuel 2"30b NKJV)!'" How do we honor God in a way that moves the hand of God? By humbling ourselves in true repentances and making Him the center and object of our very lives and our daily devotion! "What, then, shall we say in response to this? If God is for us, who can be against us? He who did not spare His own Son, but gave Him up for us all—how will He not also, along with Him, graciously give us all things (Romans 8:31-32 NIV)." For the LORD God is a sun and shield; the LORD bestows favor and honor; no good thing (including, exciting covenant love relationships) does He withhold from those whose walk is blameless (Psalm 84:9-11)!" "I beseech you therefore, brethren, by the mercies of God, that you present your bodies a living sacrifice, holy, acceptable to God, which is your reasonable service. And do not be conformed to this world, (the lust of the flesh, the lust of the eye, and the pride of life---1 John 2:16) but be transformed by the renewing of your mind, that you may prove what is that good and acceptable and perfect will of God (Romans 12:1-2 NKJV)!" Amen!

Within a few weeks of meeting Peggi, I rented the cheapest apartment I could find in Smithville, Missouri. I wanted to pay off all the bills I could before she and I got married to free us up to go wherever the Lord might send us and fulfill whatever plan He had for our lives. I came across a dingy little studio apartment in downtown Smithville for chicken feed that was close to everything and right in the price range that I wanted to pay. The problem was it was so filthy I didn't know if I could stand to live there or not. It was all I could find, though, so I rented it anyway. I put everything I owned into storage except for what I needed for the apartment and then stayed there for the next eighteen months.

I spent every weekend reading books at the laundromat, and it was during that time that God began to deal with my doubts about Peggi and even blessed me with an undeniable example that with God, all things really are possible through the marriage of two of my all-time favorite heroes of the faith, Mike and Sandy MacIntosh of Horizon Christian Fellowship in San Diego, California. Mike was your classic California beach bum, acid-popping freak, while Sandy was a straitlaced college student who just happened to be the daughter of one of Forbes's 500 richest men in the world. After reading Mike's autobiography, *For the Love of Mike*, an amazing story that I would highly recommend everyone read, I could no longer say this could never happen, because it most certainly does and already has in their lives, marriage, and ministry.

You all know my history now from reading this book, so I have no need to tell you what kind of person I was—a drug-induced alcoholic and high school dropout with nothing at all good to say about myself before I knew Jesus Christ. Peggi, on the other hand, was an extremely intelligent, very beautiful girl who'd finished six or seven years of college with a master's degree in nursing. She is a family nurse practitioner who has never done a single thing wrong in her life in comparison to me. She never did drugs, she never drank alcohol, and she most certainly has never been to jail. That's why it took two whole years for God to prepare my heart for her; actually, it took a lifetime. When I did have an opportunity to talk to her, she was one of the sweetest persons I had ever met, but I just couldn't figure out a way to break the ice and become better friends with her.

Then not too long after leaving the church in Liberty, the Lord provided another worship leader, named Dan Daily, who is a much better musician and worship leader than I am, to take my place. And after a couple months in Saint Joseph, I felt like it was a good time to go back home to Calvary Chapel Liberty and my spiritual family. It was great to be back with my church family, and this time there was no pressure to be their worship leader; God had worked all that out for the good of everyone, and all for His glory. Work had also started to slow down some, as they had hired several new drivers, alleviating the pressure on the rest of us. It was during that time that Scott began to call on me to fill the pulpit and cover the church as he began to travel more to pastors' conferences and visit his ailing father who lived in Southern California. During that time, the entire church at Liberty had learned about Peggi and began praying for God to open the door for Peggi to know and understand the plan He had revealed to me just months earlier in Saint Joseph. Then finally, during the summer of 2008, I saw her at a baptism cookout in Maryville, Missouri, where two friends and I were playing music, and finally God provided the opportunity I had been praying for.

Peggi told me she was part of a leadership team for a singles ministry in Saint Joseph and that they were in the market for some new activities for their group. I learned that her first husband, Tony, had died suddenly from a massive heart attack at age thirty-eight and that she had her son, Michael, still living at home. He was a senior in high school and severely troubled by the sudden loss of his father. Who wouldn't be? I also learned that she had absolutely no interest in dating anyone for any reason until he

was out of school and on his own, and maybe not even
then. The only man she had any interest in was Jesus
Christ, whom she considered her eternal husband and
best friend! The only reason she was involved with the
singles ministry was for fellowship and to help orga-
nize their group activities. Nevertheless the Bible says:
*"For this is contained in scripture: 'Behold, I lay in Zion
a choice stone, a precious corner stone, and he who believes in Him will not be disappointed (1 Peter 2:6).'"*

14. A Christian Love Story

When I got home that night, I had an idea for a combined outreach that I thought we might be able to do together. I decided to give her a call to see if they would want to partner with the Dry Bones Praise Band and do a special outreach for the singles ministry, only open it up to a few married couples, as well. She thought it sounded like an awesome idea and said she would bring it up at their next leadership meeting. They, too, thought it was a great idea and even had the perfect place to do it, the Midland Ministry Youth Center in South Saint Joseph.

Tom and I immediately went to work on the event and invited several friends to play in the band, then scheduled the outreach for October 25, 2008. In the weeks leading up to the outreach, the Lord began to press on my heart to prepare a message for the outreach, and each night He would give me another portion of the message. I eventually contacted Peggi to see if she thought it would be all right for me to preach a message at the event. She said yes it was fine and that she would tell the others. The message God was giving me was in Psalm 37:3–5, which says, *"Trust in the LORD, and do good; dwell in the land, and feed on His faithfulness. Delight yourself also in the LORD; and He shall give you the desires of your heart. Commit your way to the LORD; trust also in Him, and He shall bring it to pass."* The more I thought about it, the more I believed it was a message for the single Christians who had been praying for God to bring them a helpmate. I felt like the Lord was instructing them, from His word, to do all the above and then wait patiently upon the Lord to bring it to pass. In my heart, I knew I had been praying the very same thing, only for Peggi.

I had spent many nights leading up to the outreach praying for God to anoint me with His Spirit and give me His words to speak. I asked God to give Peggi eyes to see only Him at work in me to accomplish His divine purpose and that if this truly was His plan for us to be together, He would open her heart and eyes as well. Finally I asked Him to ensure that if she were going to be attracted to anything about me, it would be Jesus in me. The Lord did not disappoint. God had done far more exceedingly above all I had asked or even imagined for that night, as young people and old alike, married and singles, were flat out on their faces before the Lord, crying rivers of tears as God began to speak into their hearts. I had never felt such a strong presence of the Lord at any other time in my life. The building was packed, and God had truly opened the windows of heaven over that place to rain down His love on every person there. I remember looking at Peggi during the message as she was walking past an aisle toward the back of the room and saw her wiping tears from her face and eyes, and I remember thinking, "God, you have done it. You have touched every heart here tonight, including hers." I knew God was working this whole thing out according to the plan He had revealed to me two years before. After that night, I truly did believe God would grant me the desires of my own heart and bring it all to pass exactly as He said He would do.

After the outreach concluded, people hung around for a long time afterward. It was one of those special times of being in the presence of the Lord that you hoped would never end. After loading the last of our PA gear into the trailer, Peggi walked over to the trailer to thank me and then gave me a beautiful hug that I honestly hoped would never end. I must have hugged her for thirty or forty seconds. I really don't know. I just know it seemed like a long time. She told me later that she knew something was up after that hug, she just didn't know what. I found out later the next night that October 26 was her birthday, and I hated it that I never got to tell her happy birthday and sing her a song. Although she did request a song for her friend whose birthday was the next day, according to her, so maybe it was really for herself? The song was "I Can Only Imagine" by Mercy Me, and the whole place was singing the song.

A week later, Sunday, November 2, just happened to be my birthday, which is exactly seven days after Peggi's. I was invited to lead worship at a small church in my hometown of Stanberry, and on the way home, I started to pray that if she really was the girl I was supposed to marry, and we really were called of God for that purpose, that she would call me on the phone and wish me a happy birthday. Peggi had never called me prior to that time, and it was my understanding that she never really called any guys for reasons other than work or ministry. However, when I got home and settled in, my phone rang and it was Peggi, wishing me a happy birthday and asking how church had gone in Stanberry. She said she had thought about coming but had not been invited so decided not to go.

We talked for over three hours that night, and it was the most exciting and wonderful birthday of my life. We talked about everything from work to church, music and ministry, and even the struggles she was having with her kids, whom she loves with all her heart and was so worried about. Then she asked about my personal testimony. She had heard about my testimony from friends and insisted I share it with her. I was extremely apprehensive about talking to her about it for fear of how she might react. I didn't want to say anything that might jeopardize our friendship. One night I even had a dream that my life was at war and everyone was trying to destroy me, but for some reason I turned around and there was Peggi, arms opened wide, telling me to come to her and everything would be fine. I ran into her arms and immediately the storm passed and I was safe. I wanted to know that comfort for real more than anything and was terrified of telling her about my past. Then I remembered the Mike and Sandy MacIntosh story and decided to go all in and tell her everything she wanted to know. I thought, "Lord, this is it. You're either with me or You're not, but either way, at this point I have to know for sure."

I told her everything you just read in this book and held nothing back. To my amazement, the very thing I was the most afraid of turned out to be the one thing she loves the most about me, my testimony. She said she knew this could never have happened apart from a radical conversion followed by numerous miracles from God. After that night, we talked every night on the phone, way into the late-night hours, sometimes until our cell phone batteries ran completely down and we had to plug them into the wall to finish our conversations. She must have had a million questions about my, for lack of words, burning-bush experience and what it must have been like talking to God and all the events that followed my Jesus encounter, wanting to live each of those experiences herself.

Even today she still asks, "What was it like to talk to God and experience all those things?" Elijah is the one person that always comes to mind when someone asks me that question. Elijah heard "the still small voice of the Lord" speaking to him from inside the cave in his time of desperation, ministering to his deepest needs and instructing him in the way he should go. I have never heard the audible sound of God's voice speaking to me, but His message can be heard loud and clear without ever hearing the sound of His audible voice. You just need ears to hear and a heart to receive what the Spirit of the Lord is saying to your spirit. But say God did speak directly to you in an audible voice, or even went as far as coming into the living room of your home, sitting down, and speaking to you face-to-face and, like me, offered you a hope and a future beyond your wildest dreams, it would profit you nothing if it wasn't united together with and received by faith. "*So then faith comes by hearing, and hearing by the word of God. (Romans 10:17).*"

I really don't know what makes my life differ-ent than most, but I can assure you of this: God is no respecter of man. He loves all people the same, and the ground is level at the foot of the cross. What He did for me, He can easily do for you, too, as long as you walk according to the principles outlined in His Holy Word. That does not mean God is here to serve us and that our every wish is His command, but make Christ the center and object of your life's devotion and these promises are yours! *"These things I have written to you who believe in the name of the Son of God* [Jesus Christ], *in order that you may know that you have eternal life. And this is the confidence which we have before Him, that if we ask anything according to His will, He hears us. And if we know that He hears in whatever we ask, we know that we have the requests which we have asked from Him (1 John 5:13–15)."*

Well, at that point I was confident that Peggi not only had serious feelings for me but that it was just a matter of time before she and I were a done deal and wearing each other's wedding bands. Our friendship was rapidly growing by the day, and I was hopelessly in love with her. Then, one Thursday afternoon while running my Estes route in Saint Joseph, Peggi called me at work all upset and crying uncontrollably. I asked her what was wrong, and she told me she was scared and really didn't want to have a relationship at that time. She had promised her son she would wait until after he graduated from high school to get involved with anyone, if she even did then, but had let her guard down and violated the covenant she had made. She asked me not to call her again and said she was sorry for any heartache she may have caused me. I told her I understood and asked her if I could pray with her before she hung up. She agreed, so we prayed and then parted ways. I don't have words to describe how I felt when she said goodbye and hung up the phone. It was bad, though, I can tell you that much. I couldn't believe we were through. I never slept a wink that night and prayed my heart out to God that she would call me once her son had graduated and things were different.

The next day was horrible, just trying to get through work with no sleep and still sick from the night before and not being able to talk to Peggi anymore. However, I was about to learn a valuable lesson about the opposite sex, how girls can be extremely strange and moody creators when they're falling in love; things can sometimes make absolutely no sense whatsoever! I got through work and headed for home, hoping to be able to eat something and get some sleep. At least the next day was the weekend and I didn't have to work. I thought perhaps I might feel better Monday.

However, the minute I walked in the door at home, my phone rang and it was Peggi. "Hey, how's everything going?" I thought to myself, "Are you serious?" I said, "Not good, Peggi; I didn't sleep a wink last night. Don't you remember our conversation yesterday?" She said, "Yes, but I don't feel that way anymore. Can't we still be friends?" I was so confused but at the same time relieved. I was just happy to hear from her again and be able to talk to her. By the end of the weekend, we were back to where we left off, talking for hours on end without any weird feelings of any kind or any confusion. It was great to have my friend back.

Then the next week she called and asked me point-blank, "Why do you want to talk to me all the time, and what exactly is your interest in me?" I had not told her what I believed God had said about the two of us, but she insisted before we go any further I tell her everything that was on my mind, so that's just what I did. It didn't come as any shock to her, though, by that time. She knew I had fallen in love and figured that's what I had in mind. She didn't say yes, but she didn't say no either. After that discussion, I was feeling very confident about our future together. But then Wednesday came around and I remembered the previous Thursday and thought, "What are the chances of something like that happening again?"

Well, the next day the phone rang, and once again it was Peggi, all upset and crying uncontrollably just like the week before.

She told me she thought she was past all those negative emotions, but apparently she wasn't, and this time she said, "I am serious; we can't talk anymore!" She asked me not to call her again and again apologized for whatever heartache she had caused me. I thought it was for real this time, and again I couldn't sleep a wink that whole night. I just sat there at home, pouring my heart out to God, trying to make sense of it all. Maxie just happened to call that night, and even though I really didn't feel like talking, I asked her if she would pray for me because it was really hard at that time. She was more than happy to pray for me and talk to me as long as I needed. She reminded me that God was in control and that she believed everything would work out for the best. I was so thankful for her friendship that night and felt much better after we talked.

The Lord calmed me down after Maxie and I talked and even managed to restore most of my peace about Peggi and me. The next night I got off work and headed for the house, hoping to be able to get some sleep. However, the second I walked through the door, the phone rang. It was Peggi. "Hey, Ellis, how are you doing?" I thought, "You've got to be kidding." I said,

"Not good at all. How am I supposed to be? Do you remember our conversation from yesterday?" She said yes but said she was all right now and wanted to remain friends if I still wanted to. Well, of course I did, and like the week before, I was just relieved to hear from her again. Then when the following Thursday came around, it happened again just like the previous Thursdays. I finally figured out it only happened on Thursdays, so when the following Wednesday rolled around, I asked, "Peg, can we not talk tomorrow? I'll call you Friday. I can't take another Thursday meltdown!" She told me not to worry that there would be no more Thursday meltdowns and we could talk Thursday. This time she was right; we made it through our first Thursday without her going to pieces. In fact, she asked me out on our first date together for the following weekend, which turned out to be the time of our lives. We had met numerous times at Hazel's Coffee House where we talked for hours on end and drank coffee, all the while growing closer and closer and both falling hopelessly in love with the other. This time we were going on a real date together, roller-skating. I wasn't much of a roller-skater, but it was great fun with her.

The following week she called me at two o'clock in the morning all excited, explaining that she had been having all this trouble with our relationship until

God instructed her to read Psalm 37. She told me she had been committed to a five-year plan given to her by her closest friend, Rhonda Schram, from the book of Leviticus that God had instructed her to abide by and that's why she wouldn't get involved with anyone; it all had to do with the long-term good of both her and her two children. However, God had directed her to read Psalm 37, and she wanted to know if that meant anything to me. I asked her if she remembered the message from October 25, that it was from Psalm 37. She said she did not remember the message because of a Catholic girl sitting in the back row of the church at the outreach. She thought the girl was a little overwhelmed by the undeniable presence of the Lord in the house that night. We learned that she was not used to all the hands rising and modern worship music and was feeling uncomfortable and a little out of place, so Peggi spent most of the evening at the back of the sanctuary praying for that girl. Psalm 37 ultimately became Biblical marital confirmation for both of us, only in two completely different ways. The five-year plan made perfect sense, as God would want her to allow for plenty of time for both her and her kids to heal before getting involved with someone else. God was looking after her as only He can do, while at the same time preparing her for the journey that lay ahead for both of us. The passage that was Leviticus (19:23–25) also turned out to be the blueprint for the ministry God had prepared for us. Her friend, Rhonda, also told her she would be marrying a pastor, or in other words, someone called of God for the ministry, and it would be confirmed in the written Word of God. And what Peggi hadn't taken into account was the fact that she had almost completed the fourth year already by the time we started talking and was beginning her fifth year in just a few short days; in other words she was already there. *"And when you enter that land and plant all kinds of trees for food, then you shall count their fruit as forbidden. Three years it shall be forbidden to you; it shall not be eaten. But in the fourth year all its fruit shall be holy, an offering of praise to the LORD. And in the fifth year you are to eat of its fruit, that its yield may increase for you; I am the LORD your God (Leviticus 19:23–25)."*

Things moved pretty fast after that, and we were married on February 14, 2009, Valentine's Day, in the very church where it all began for me many years before—Calvary Chapel Saint Joseph, and my dad was my best man. It was a beautiful wedding and the church was packed. It was the greatest day of my life apart from March 6, 1997, when I surrendered my life to Jesus, and, thank God, Thursdays were now over for good.

Between my wonderful church families, Estes Express, my personal family, including Peggi's, and now Peggi herself, God had indeed fulfilled His promise to restore all the love that was ever taken from my life and, in the words of Pastor Mike MacIntosh of Horizon Christian Fellowship, "I am a complete salvation in Jesus Christ my Lord!" *"The LORD is my shepherd; I shall not want. He makes me to lie down in green pastures; He leads me besides still waters. He restores my soul; He leads me in the path of righteousness For His name's sake. Yea, though I walk through the valley of the shadow of death, I will fear no evil; for You are with me; Your rod and Your staff, they comfort me. You prepare a table before me in the presence of my enemies; You anoint my head with oil; my cup runs over. Surely goodness and mercy shall follow me all the days of my life; and I will dwell in the house of the LORD forever, Amen (Psalm 23:1–6)!"*

15. Go into All the World

Shortly after Peggi and I were married, some friends and we formed a board of directors and decided to incorporate the ministry Tom, John, and I had started several years before. Tom was married just months before Peggi and me, and soon thereafter he, too, quit the band to settle down and enjoy the married life and to better serve his own church in his hometown of Stewartsville, Missouri. The ministry, however, continued to grow even after he left the group, with a new generation of young musicians traveling with us from church to church. It was such a blessing to watch those young people growing in the Lord and using their talents for His glory, and the churches loved them. The ministry had become Peggi's and my passion as God continued to open doors for us to serve Him in the evangelistic arena of ministry, and in the spring of 2009, we filed our letter of intent for the corporation and within two months had completed all the necessary steps.

We were officially registered and approved as a Missouri 501c3 nonprofit ministry under the name of His Song Evangelistic Outreach Ministries. Shortly after it was completed, Peggi and I decided it was finally time to skip town and go on a long -overdue honeymoon vacation. We were both so busy that we had to postpone our honeymoon until the summer. We headed north to visit her sister and a pastor friend of mine who both live in Minot, North Dakota, before heading south to the Black Hills of South Dakota to visit Spearfish, Deadwood, and, of course, beautiful Mount Rushmore. That trip would be the doorway into the future for Peggi and me and would soon have us packing our belongings back home and moving westward to gorgeous Spearfish, South Dakota, where we would live for the next eighteen months.

During our visit to Spearfish, we came across a husband and wife, Marty and Debra Hogan, who were starting a new church inside an old run-down amphitheater where the *Passion Play* had been reenacted for the past seventy years. Wow, what a place to start a new church! During our initial conversation, we discovered we all had roots in Calvary Chapel. They, however, were with a Four Square Church at the time that had sent them there to plant a Four Square Church in Spearfish.

They had come across the amphitheater through a realtor in the area who allowed them access to the property to start the church and raise money to purchase and renovate the property. The view was spectacular, but the place had sat empty for several years and was in need of work. The owners were asking five million dollars for the property, but no one could figure out how to make a business profitable or purchase the property at that price. Apparently, attendance had dropped off dramatically for the *Passion Play*, and they simply couldn't afford the overhead to keep the production running any longer. It cost a fortune to take care of the grounds and all the animals, not to mention the actors and actresses.

Marty, however, had a degree in theatrical production and thought he could resurrect it from the dead and make it work again. They were given so many months to schedule a number of fund-raiser events, such as Christian concerts and theatrical productions, in an attempt to raise enough cash for the initial down payment to purchase the amphitheater, while fixing the place up at the same time.

When we asked them about the possibility of doing an evangelistic outreach there, they jumped at the opportunity to partner with us and offered the venue for free if we would help them raise funds for the property. They said they would provide the venue, a team of trained volunteers, and all the food vendors if we would assemble and bring in a notable ministry team for the outreach. Instead of charging admission, we would receive free will offerings at each scheduled event in hopes of drawing more people to the event, then after all the expenses were covered, we would donate the rest to the property fund. We agreed to do some research to see who would come and what the cost would be and then pray for God's will and direction.

Peggi and I finished our honeymoon and headed back to Missouri to do some research, and to my surprise, there were several different ministries willing to assemble and travel hundreds of miles to do the outreach with us, and all that most of them asked for was that we cover their expenses. Within two weeks, Marty called and said they were all in for the event if we were. I told him to count us in and give us a time to schedule the event. We settled on the final weekend of July 2010 and called the outreach "Celebration Life Festival & Crusade." We jumped in with both oars and headed straight for deep waters. I had never done an event of that caliber before and didn't know the first thing about putting something like that together. However, I had a good friend in Missouri named David Lin who did. Dave is founder of the Nehemiah Festival, the biggest independent Christian music festival in the Midwest, and he had all the know-how and connections to pull this outreach together. Dave introduced me to Bread of Stone, a young Christian rock band from Iowa that had toured with many of the biggest Christian bands in the world. They were the headline band for the Nehemiah Fest but also did production for the main stage each year. Dave put me in touch with them, and they agreed to do the event. David is also lead singer for the band 9th Hour, another Christian rock band based in Smithville, Missouri, and they also agreed to come. I had a close friend in California, Pastor Justin Alfred. Justin was cohost of a national call-in radio program called *To Every Man an Answer*. Justin said he would be honored to speak at the event, as well. We invited Dr. George Westlake, a notable author and Bible teacher from Sheffield Family Life Center in Kansas City, Missouri, who cohosted a call-in television program for twenty-five years with his wife and had taught in Bible colleges all over the world. George accepted our invitation as well. Next we invited Shawn Derritt of Christ Inner Healing Ministries in Shawnee, Kansas, and Jeremy Riddle, a nationally known worship artist from Redding, California.

The event was scheduled almost a year in advance to give us plenty of time to prepare, but people began to hear about the event early. Then one afternoon while driving my Estes route in Saint Joseph, I received a call from a girl in Spearfish, South Dakota, asking if I was with Calvary Chapel. I told her that I attended a Calvary Chapel in Missouri for a number of years and that I had been involved with Calvary Chapel most of my Christian life. She then asked about the outreach and if we would consider coming to Spearfish and starting a Calvary Chapel. For years I had sensed God's calling for me to start a fellowship, but was this the time? I told her we would certainly pray about it and thanked her for her interest in the outreach. The next week she called again and said there were even more people who wanted us to come and start a Calvary Chapel Bible study.

Well, after another couple of phone calls, Peggi and I decided to take a weekend and at least drive out there and meet them. I was honored by their invitation for us to come and lead them in a Bible study, and it would give me a chance to visit with Marty at the amphitheater and discuss our upcoming event. We told her we would come and meet them and have lunch with them in a couple weeks. She was extremely excited, and the next week she called again and said there was a city-owned building downtown that had been used in the past for starting another church, and the city said we could use it for absolutely no charge at all to do a Bible study while we were in town. Two weeks later, we drove 705 miles one way to lead a Bible study for a girl and her friends whom we had never met before in our lives. It was exciting, though, and when we got there, nine people came out for the Bible study. When we finished, they asked us if we would come back and do it again, but only this time, to live and start a new church. They all offered to help with the Celebration Life Festival & Crusade and would even help move us if we decided to live there.

On the way back home to Missouri, Peggi and I both began to feel like God was pressing on our hearts to take that leap of faith and move to South Dakota. We both believed with all our hearts that God wanted us to go. Two weeks later, we went back to Spearfish and led the Bible study again, and every two weeks after that for the next two and a half months. Then finally, after two and a half months of driving back and forth 705 miles one way for church on Sunday, we packed everything we owned and moved to Spearfish, South Dakota, to oversee the Bible study God had started there.

However, just before we left, the most wonderful thing you could ever imagine happened. I had made a very dear friend named Jeremy Thornton, who was manager of the shipping department at Enterprise Manufacturing in Saint Joseph. My company had been making daily pickups there for a little over two years, and Jeremy and I became very good friends during that time. I had the opportunity to share Jesus with him and his brother-in-law, James, on many occasions. They were both awesome guys, always willing to stay late to make sure we got our shipments picked up and do anything they could to make our lives as drivers easier. I thought the world of both of them and even bought them both Bibles to read at home and study the things we would discuss throughout the week. Both guys would listen to every word I had to say with the utmost respect, and both were full of questions from time to time. I could sense God working in all our lives many times when we would talk about Israel and other world events and how it all lined up with scripture. Peggi and I would pray for them both daily, hoping that one day we would have the opportunity to witness them inviting Jesus Christ into their hearts.

Then just weeks before we left for South Dakota, Jeremy and I were the only two there at the end of the day, and we began to discuss Christ's second coming. I could tell Jeremy had some serious questions on his heart that he wanted to take care of and soon, so I asked him if he wanted to receive Jesus into his life. Before our conversation was over, we were standing in the back of my Estes Express Lines trailer, heads bowed before the Lord, while Jeremy asked Jesus Christ to come into his heart. It was an indescribable moment that I will never forget as long as I live, and Jeremy,

I'm proud of you, bro. I'm honored to call you my friend—you, too, James. I had always regretted the fact that I didn't have enough time before we moved to help Jeremy get grounded in his faith, but when I visited him in 2012 on a trip to Missouri, I discovered that God must have taken care of that Himself, as Jeremy was still just as excited three years later as he was the day we shook hands and said goodbye.

Immediately after Jeremy's conversion, Peggi and I left for good. It was the end of one chapter of our lives and the beginning of another. *"He who is holy, who is true, who has the key of David, who opens and no one will shut, and who shuts and no one opens, says this: 'I know your deeds. Behold, I have put before you an open door which no one can shut, because you have a little power, and have kept My word, and have not denied My name. (Revelation 3:7–8).'"* Peggi and I lived in South Dakota for a year and half, teaching the word of God, doing the Celebration Life Festival & Crusade, and even opening a ministry center that housed a college and young-adult ministry called "the River" that would run between 80 to 120 kids each week. Young Life met there on Monday nights, and a team of adults that made up an Ethiopian mission team, called "Look Development," met there every Tuesday night. They coordinated mission trips and fund-raisers to help develop a twenty-acre piece of land in Shone, Ethiopia, to house orphans and widows in the area, and a hospital along with a school to help educate the underserved children of Shone.

It was an awesome year and a half that will stay with us for the rest of our lives. The biggest problem we ran into was when Marty and Debra Hogan were told they were out of time and would need to evacuate the amphitheater for lack of funds, leaving us without a venue for the Celebration Life Festival & Crusade. It turned out to be a minor setback, though, as the Black Hills State University opened their facility for us to do the outreach there.

We made several lifelong friends while in South Dakota, and one whom is a His Song board member. But then after a year and a half there, we knew the Lord was telling us our time in South Dakota was over and it was time to go. After doing a lot of soul searching and praying for direction, we moved to beautiful Colorado Springs, Colorado, where we found another wonderful church home and family at the Calvary Worship Center with Pastor Al Pittman, one of the best Bible teachers of our generation. It's also the church Justin Alfred served at before he and Janie moved to Southern California. His Song Evangelistic Outreach Ministries is also based in Colorado Springs, where we sponsor another ministry called Sets Captives Free Ministry, along with their thirty-two-acre therapy horse ranch located in nearby Green Mountain Falls, Colorado, called Victory to Freedom Ranch, a ministry that's run by women for women getting out of prison, an awesome ministry that's very dear to my heart for many reasons. You can read all about Victory to Freedom Ranch and many other exciting endeavors the Lord has blessed us with on this remarkable journey by visiting our website posted in the back of the book. We now have board of directors and ministry members scattered all over the Midwest, including South Dakota and Missouri. And as of the writing of this book, there are numerous Celebration Life Festival & Crusade outreaches scheduled for multiple states and even more in the works, God willing. We are 100 percent committed to go wherever the Lord sends us to preach the gospel message and be at His disposal to help set the captives free, reaching as many unsaved people for Jesus Christ as possible with whatever time on this Earth we have left.

And before I conclude this book and say my good-byes, I would like to invite you to send us your prayer requests via the His Song website; it would be an honor and privilege to pray for you. Also, like us on facebook and sign up for our monthly newsletter. And then please let us know what you thought of this book; I hope it has been a blessing and an encouragement for you to read. I hope it has shined the light of God's eternal hope and glory into your lives, as well, so that you, too, can clearly see and know for yourselves that nothing is impossible with God when we surrender our lives in full to Him. Finally, no book like this would be complete without a personal invitation for you to receive Jesus Christ as your own personal Lord and Savior and find answers, as well as guidance, for your own spiritual journeys. The book was written with my utmost desire to bring hope, strength, and healing to countless lives and families everywhere, and it's my deepest heartfelt prayer that all you who read this book will be able to look through the eternal lens of God and see the beauty of your own master portrait and all that you can be as His workmanship created in Christ Jesus, by the Potter's hands! *"For I am confident of this very thing, that He who began a good work in you will perfect it until the day of Christ Jesus (Philippians 1:6)."*

16. Will You Say "Yes" to Jesus Christ?

I spent nearly half my life full of bitter hatred that left me alone, hopeless, and bankrupt of any real purpose at all in life. No one could do anything for me until Jesus Christ came into my life on March 6, 1997, created in me a new heart, and gave me a hope and a future and a brand-new beginning in Him. My whole purpose in life now is to share the hope of Jesus Christ and the cross on which He died to pay the debt for your sins and mine to set us, the captives, free.

No matter what your current situation is or what nationalities you may be, I want you to know that Jesus Christ loves you. He desires to give you life, and life more abundantly, if you will just trust Him completely this day. As I said in the beginning of the book, there are absolutely no lives beyond God's infinite passion and desire to love and to know, and absolutely no situation, pain, sin, or failure beyond His infinite desire and ability to forgive, heal, and restore if you will trust Him and obey. If you will read the scriptures below and believe them with all your heart, pray the prayer below, confess your sins, and ask Jesus to come into your life, this very day you, too, will be a new creation in Jesus Christ, ready for the Potter's wheel, and I would like to be the first to welcome you into the Family of God. Amen!

Mark 2:17—Jesus said He did not come to call the righteous, but sinners, to repentance.

John 3:16—God so loved the whole world that He gave His only begotten Son, that whoever believes in Him should not perish but have everlasting life.

Romans 3:23—All have sinned and fallen short of the glory of God.

Romans 6:23—The wages of sin is death, but the gift of God is eternal life in Christ Jesus our Lord.

Romans 10:9—If you confess with your mouth the Lord Jesus and believe in your heart that God has raised Him from the dead, you will be saved.

1 John 5:13—These things I have written to you who believe in the name of the Son of God, in order that you may know that you have eternal life.

1 John 1:9—If we confess our sins, He is faithful and righteous to forgive us our sins and to cleanse us from all unrighteousness.

"Today, if you hear His voice, do not harden your hearts." Hebrews 4:7

The Bible says that now is the acceptable time; today is the day of salvation. Tomorrow's not promised to anyone. If you would like to receive the gift of eternal life, first you must believe in the Lord Jesus Christ. You must ask for your sin to be forgiven and then put your trust in Him. John 14:6 says there is no other way to heaven except through Jesus Christ. If you want to begin a personal relationship with Jesus Christ, you can begin by praying this prayer: "Father God, I confess I am a sinner, and God I am sorry for my sin. With your help I want to turn from my sin and to Jesus Christ, the only begotten Son of God, and ask that my sin be forgiven, that wonderful times of refreshing may come to me from the presence of the Lord (Acts 3:19). Today I receive Jesus as my personal Lord and Savior and confess His Holy name. From now on, I want to follow Jesus wherever He leads, live for Him, and worship Him and Him alone. I pray these things in Jesus' name. Amen."

Visit us online at:

http://www.hissongevangelism.org

or

http://www.celebrationlifefestival.com

½ Price Books

$2.⁰⁰ 07/29/15